WHEN THE
MIRACLE
DOESNT HAPPEN

~HOW TO SURVIVE LOSS AND FIND PURPOSE IN THE PAIN~

~JALESA HENEKE~

This book is a memoir. It reflects the author's present recollections of experiences over time. Some names have been changed, some events have been compressed, and some dialogue has been recreated.

DEDICATION

"Use all the gifts God gave you."
"When God gives you an idea, do it. Because if you don't, He'll give it to someone else."
– Words of wisdom from my beautiful mother.

You always told me I could do anything, and writing was one of the many gifts you encouraged me to use. I'm not surprised that an idea inspired by you is what finally pushed me out of my comfort zone to write this book. This is for you, Mom, Christine Clark Lowe.

CONTENTS

INTRODUCTION

No one likes to talk about death. As humans we shy away from the topic as if by talking about it, we'll somehow shorten our own lives. It isn't until death touches our lives in a personal way that we are forced to come to terms with it.

When my mother passed, death threw my entire world upside down, leaving me shaken to my core. It was the first time that I had a front row seat to experiencing grief. I had experienced death in my family, but never someone this close to me. I remember the passing of my great grandfather when I was child: even when I stood at his casket and touched his cold hard cheek at the wake, my mind didn't fully grasp the gravity of the situation. Over the years, I attended some funerals and while I sympathized for those who lost a loved one, I didn't truly understand the pain they were going through.

As a teenager and an avid reader, I experienced the threat of death through books. In the summers, I would ride my bike to the neighborhood library and spend hours searching the shelves for books to take home. If I found one I really liked, I'd find a quiet corner to get cozy in and dive into worlds and characters that fascinated me. One author in particular grabbed my attention thoroughly: Lurlene Mc-Daniel wrote books about teenagers and young adults who fought cancer and terminal illnesses. At the time, my mother thought it was strange I liked reading about these things, but I was fascinated by the characters and their strength. It amazed me how these young characters dared to live despite their illness and how much their strength impacted those around them. My mother couldn't understand why something that she considered to be depressing had made such an impression on me. Now, I believe God was preparing me all those years ago for my own mother's diagnosis.

It was April 2019 when she was diagnosed with acute leukemia. I remember feeling my stomach drop completely when she told me the news. I had no idea how to react.

Do I scream and rage? Do I hide in fear? Do I pretend that everything is okay? I didn't know what to do.

There is no manual on how to handle that kind of news. That's when I thought back on those books that kept me company and fascinated me in my adolescence. Back then, I had no clue that I would one day face a similar tribulation. But God did. The pain and anguish of what they went through and those they left behind, but also the determination and love spoke so loudly to me. I wanted to be the person in my mother's corner that gave her hope and inspired her like those characters did for me.

Mom had the softest cheeks. When I hugged her, she would press her cheek to mine in a way that made it feel like everything would be okay, like she was my shield protecting me from harm, and I loved rubbing her cheek with mine in contentment. It's those small moments that I miss the most. To know that I will never hear her voice again, never see her smile, never feel her hugs, never hear her loud laughter, never get her advice and wisdom. The sheer pain of losing someone so near and dear to you is something that can never be described, as there are no words.

My mother was and still is a vital part of me, so much

so that sometimes I can almost feel her. It's amazing how our minds can hold such vivid memories of our loved ones, and when the mind pairs with grief, it can play some beautiful yet cruel games on us. After a year without her, I began to experience dreams of her still being alive. They were so real my husband had to wake me up because I was sobbing in my sleep. The most heartbreaking dream I had was my mother being present for the birth of my first-born child, something I wished had actually happened. The dream was beautiful because I was with her again, but waking up was cruel because I realized all over again that she was gone.

Experiencing loss is brutal. Don't let anyone fool you. In the beginning, there were times when I cried so much from missing my mother that I felt like I couldn't breathe. That's how much the pain would weigh me down. But every day is a fresh start, and I've found ways to keep living and honor her.

My mother left too soon. She was only fifty-eight, and she had dreams to live a great life. *We* had dreams to live a great life. Plans to write a book telling her story in hopes of helping others. Traveling the world as missionaries. Family events, vacationing in Greece, and spending time with her future grandchildren. But now I must live out those dreams without her because I know that's what she would want me to do. As much as I want to curl up in a ball and lie in bed on the days when I'm feeling miserable and miss her the most, I refuse to do that.

I want to face grief head on. I admit that I allow myself a moment at times to cry when it feels almost unbearable; however, I find the will to keep going. Hiding from our pain doesn't make it suddenly disappear. It is meant to be dealt with so that we can better not only ourselves but those around us. I owe my determination to my mother because in watching her grieve the loss of *her* mother, she taught me that life keeps going despite the pain and that I can always find a place of comfort in God.

My faith in God has always been a running theme in my life. Because I grew up in church, some would say that Christianity is something that I was obligated to believe in, but as I got older, I began to grow into my faith. In a world that doesn't make much sense at times, God and my faith have kept me afloat when I felt I was drowning in a sea of chaos. It's not a religion, but a very real and tangible relationship with God.

I never thought I would write a book, no matter how much my mother thought I would be good at it. And I'm not cocky enough to think that this was all my idea. In fact, I know this book was not my idea. It very clearly came from God. This is a labor of tears, pain, and ultimately love. In writing this book, I found hidden regrets, uncovered denials, and acknowledged some ugly truths. But as I share my grief journey with you, I pray that you find comfort in knowing you're not alone and there is strength in sharing that pain with others.

In these pages you will find a kindred soul. I won't judge you for the thoughts you may never speak out loud because there's a chance that I had those same thoughts. At the end of each chapter, you will have an opportunity to face your pain head-on and answer some of the questions you've been too afraid to ask yourself. Journaling is a cathartic experience that can help free your mind if you let it. You won't get your answers all at once, but maybe this can be the beginning of healing your pain. I hope that in some small way this book can be the encouragement you need to survive whatever loss you have experienced and trust God when the miracle doesn't happen.

CHAPTER 1

A LOVE LIKE NO OTHER

*"No daughter and mother ever live apart,
no matter what the distance between them."*
— Christie Watson

One of my earliest and fondest memories is my mother singing the song "You Are My Sunshine" with me as a child. As the day would come to end, she would sit me on her lap and hug me to her as she gently rocked me in her arms before going to bed. It was our time to just be. A safe cocoon meant only for two. Even as I got older into adulthood, Mom insisted that we sing that song together. I was always a headstrong child that was constantly on the move and never liked to be bored so it was hard for her to keep me occupied unless she stuck a book in my face. However, in those moments when we sang "You Are My Sunshine" together, I would settle down for a few minutes, usually with my cheek pressed to hers and experience a certain peace that only a loving mother can bring to her child. Even into adulthood, when we found pockets of time to just be and she would laughingly encourage me to sing what had become our song, I knew that I was wholeheartedly loved. So when my world was completely shaken, in some ways it didn't matter because I had a love that burned bright, and I poured every ounce of it back into her.

BLINDSIDED

Over the years, my mother and I shared many tender and fun moments with each other. From singing "You Are My Sunshine" together to attending concerts together. We saw Chris Brown, John Legend, and Justin Timberlake. My mom was fun to hang out with! We developed a bond that was as intricate and tightly woven as a precious blanket. She would affectionately say, "We gonna ride this thing (life) till the wheels fall off!" She was not only my mother, but she had become a best friend and my number one confidante. I like to think she thought of me the same way. When you develop such a tight bond, there's not much that slips your notice, so I was blindsided, to say the least, when my mother called with shocking news.

"Jalesa," she said, her tone too serious to be good news. "For the past few months, I've been going to the doctor for a condition and I was recently diagnosed."

"What?" I asked, my mouth dry. "What do you mean a condition? What diagnosis? Mom, what's going on?"

"I've been diagnosed with Myelodysplastic Syndrome," she said all in one breath.

As my mother said that she had been experiencing unexplained bruises on her body for a few months, my heart began to pound in my chest.

"I didn't see any bruises while I was home," I said as

I was trying to wrap my brain around what my mother was telling me.

"I covered them up with makeup because I didn't want you to worry during your wedding," she said.

It was a debilitating blow to realize that she had been holding on to something so big, but I also understood that she was trying to protect me. *My life is never going to be the same*, I thought as I got off the phone with her. I couldn't move. I couldn't talk. I couldn't think. It was as if something had shocked me out of my own body and I no longer had control of it. My life had officially moved into uncharted territory that seemed to be filled with landmines, and I had no idea where to step without blowing up my life.

It had all been going so well.

My husband Daniel and I had just celebrated our wedding in November 2018. It was also our one-year anniversary because we had made the decision to get legally married in a courthouse the previous year. But like most women, I still wanted my fairytale wedding. Mom was with me every step of the way as I planned, giving me advice on colors, tasting cakes, and finding the venue. I had this fear that we would bump heads because she had the tendency to take over things, but she managed to reel herself in (after I gave her a very stern talking to). And it helped that I put her in charge of the rehearsal dinner!

Mom was ecstatic about our wedding. "It's gonna be like a family reunion!"

Family had always been important to her and the fact that many of our loved ones would be together in one room celebrating her first-born child filled her with joy. Our wedding and reception were filled with love and laughter. The

DJ kept us dancing all night from a soul train line to my grandmother breaking out into funny little hops on the dance floor and my parents teasingly flirting as they shimmied on the floor. It was a night that most of my family and friends still fondly reminisce on to this day.

The following months continued in that same vein of joy. We experienced a wonderful honeymoon exploring the beautiful island of Puerto Rico. We had a blast immersing ourselves in the culture, so much that Daniel decided to brush off his Spanish skills. There were several times that he was actually mistaken for being Puerto Rican! As self-proclaimed foodies, we enjoyed some of the freshest lobster that burst with flavor and Daniel became obsessed with the local cuisine called mofongo. We cruised through a rain forest on ATVs and walked the historic halls of the famous Castillo San Felipe del Morro in Old San Juan. There's something about eating with your spouse on the beach as the sun sets that makes you feel like you'll never be more in love than you are in that moment. From Puerto Rico, we cruised through the Caribbean islands. We drank rum on St. Croix, sunbathed on the beaches of Barbados (the most beautiful clear waters), soaked in hot springs in Grenada, and so much more! If I were to sum up my life in one word during this time, I would choose *divine.*

Just a month later, we spent Christmas with my in-laws in Orlando. The six of us shared a two-bedroom condo. I admit I wasn't too keen on the idea of sharing space at first, but it was a great time of bonding. We ate at the popular Sugar Factory trying decadent drinks and milkshakes, explored Disney Springs, and lounged in the hot tub of our resort. On Christmas Day, his family ventured off to Walt

Disney World while we visited Universal Studios. Later that evening, we exchanged gifts. Life couldn't get any sweeter.

Until it turned into venom.

My mother sharing her diagnosis with me after having so many wonderful experiences brought everything to a screeching halt. *Why didn't she tell me?* I asked myself repeatedly.

But that was so like my mother. She always thought of others before herself. She had decided that she wanted me to experience all of life's joys during that time. I respected her greatly because even in her confusion and fear as she tried to figure out what was going on with her, she also tried her best to safeguard me during one of the happiest times of my life. Still, I was gutted when I learned that my mother was dealing with Myelodysplastic Syndrome (MDS), a pre-condition for leukemia. But at the same time, I was happy because I naively thought that she would be okay since the doctors found it early.

"An enemy has done this," the doctor told my parents.

Her body was betraying her and there was no explanation for how or why. However, we believed that God was on our side, and we would come out better and stronger as a family on the other side.

PROTECTOR OF THE HEART

As a sophomore in college, I attempted to rekindle a relationship with an old boyfriend from high school. Looking back, I was being completely ridiculous. None of the circumstances for why we previously broke up had changed, but I was hopeful and naively loved him in the only way a nineteen-year-old could. Mom never said a word to stop me. Instead, she listened as I happily talked to her about my budding romance, and she continued to listen when just a few months later I cried my heart out over my failed attempt to rekindle what I thought was love. It wouldn't be until my heart was mended that she told me she knew it wouldn't work.

"Any boy that constantly disappoints you isn't for you," she explained. "I know how much you cared about him, and you needed to try, but now you can finally move on."

She knew at the time that I probably wouldn't listen and needed to make my own decisions and mistakes. She saw my happiness in the moment and supported my decision in the ups and the unavoidable downs.

THE OTHER SHOE DROPS

Only a month after telling me about her diagnosis, my mother uttered words that would again forever alter my world.

"They couldn't stop it."

In that month, I prayed more than I had ever prayed before. For the first time, I truly learned what it meant to intercede with prayer on someone's behalf. Mom was tired. She could easily pray for herself, but she needed someone to uplift her spirits when she felt too tired to do it herself. It's like Moses needing the help of Aaron and Hur to defeat their enemies:

"Whenever Moses held up his hand, Israel prevailed, and whenever he lowered his hand, Amalek prevailed. But Moses' hands grew weary, so they took a stone and put it

under him, and he sat on it, while Aaron and Hur held up
his hands, one on one side, and the other on the other side.
So his hands were steady until the going down of the sun"
(Exodus 17:11-12).

I wanted to be the steadfastness she could rely on.

"Jalesa, can you pray for me?" she implored me one
night on the phone.

"You want me to pray for you?" I was taken aback.
My mother's prayers were powerful. She could call down
heaven to earth. I felt so inadequate, but I would never refuse
Mom this request.

"God, we trust in you," I started. "You said that you
would never give more than we can handle. This is just a
pit stop on the road of life, and we believe for healing." My
prayers were cautious at first but full of faith and hope. As
we navigated doctor's visits, medications, and uncertainty, I
learned to be more confident but also vulnerable when I talked to God. In my prayers, it never occurred to me that she
could actually develop cancer. We would be the family that
experienced a miracle, so we prayed, believed, and trusted
God, as this was just the hand we were dealt, even when
my mother had officially been diagnosed with acute myeloid
leukemia.

When you hear of other people being diagnosed with
cancer, it's hard to imagine what they must be feeling. You
say things like "I'm sorry" or maybe you pray for them when
you think of them, but ultimately your life is unaffected. But
when it's your loved one who has been diagnosed with cancer, you realize the many ways your life will never be the
same. Whatever track your life was on before, it is now de-
railed, and you are left to figure out how to make sense of

this new path you find yourself on.

LIFE'S PATHS

My life has taken quite a few paths. Some planned and others quite unexpected. In December 2014, I would leave home to go to Navy basic training in Great Lakes, Illinois. My twenty-fourth birthday was spent far from everyone and everything I loved as I suffered through the cold winter of Illinois. This was not my original plan when I graduated from college in 2012. In fact, I wanted to join the Air Force as a public relations officer. However, after being rejected by my Air Force recruiter and working jobs that were leading me nowhere for two years, I made the decision to make a major life change.

Enlisting in the Navy gave me opportunities that I had dreamed of. I studied the Arabic language, learned a new technical skill, and worked at one of the largest three-letter government agencies in the United States. My five-year career allowed me to live in California, Florida, and Maryland. And the best part of it all was meeting my husband, Daniel.

While I had a promising career ahead of me in the Navy, I recognized that the military life was not for me. I couldn't fathom letting the military dictate my life and career for twenty years. With Daniel's blessing, we agreed that I would separate to pursue my dreams and he would stay in. My mother's diagnosis came amidst my plans to start yet again on a new path. I had less than a year to finish out my service, and I was excited to start a new journey in life, which included taking time off from work and then an internship with a marketing company. But none of that mattered when it came to making sure I could be there for my mother. I had my entire year planned out, but I began to rearrange those plans immediately.

I can only imagine what it must have felt like for my mother and father to get that news. The struggle to come to terms with her diagnosis, the uncertainty and fear and the questions she must have been asking God. But she showed a quiet strength that I always admired. There was no anger. She simply went to God in prayer and determined that she would fight this enemy.

"Jalesa, I still have work to do. God isn't through with me yet," Mom declared to me one day. She was determined that she would beat the odds. "I've heard stories of people being miraculously healed. Maybe that can happen for me too."

Her hope sparked mine, and so we joined together as a family in our belief that she would be healed. We were careful with our words and how we phrased things.

"Your mother doesn't *have* cancer, Jalesa," my dad told me. "She's been diagnosed with it. Words have power, and we're not taking ownership of this cancer."

I took my cue from them and prepared to go to battle with her. However, I did not expect how much she would come to rely on me.

"Mom, have you talked to Josh?" I asked her one day, though I felt as if I already knew her answer: No, she didn't tell my younger brother. He'd always been her baby, and she just couldn't bring herself to tell him about the diagnosis and break his heart.

Joshua and I couldn't be more different. With seven years between us, I've always been an emotionally tough person who never shies away from brutal honesty, while my brother prefers a more loving approach.

"Do you want me to tell him for you?" I asked my mom. There was a pause on the phone as she considered my question. "He needs to know."

She sighed heavily and then said, "I know he needs to know . . . It's just that I can't bring myself to tell him."

"You can't keep him in the dark, Mom," I insisted. "I'll tell him."

This time she sighed with relief as she replied, "Yes, please."

Why does it have to fall on me? It should be her. I couldn't help but think. But despite my frustration, I agreed.

"Okay, Mom," I said.

How do you tell your unsuspecting sibling such devastating news? It was like a weight sitting on my chest as I called him. I almost didn't want him to answer the phone. If only just to give myself a little more time to figure out how to tell him. But Mom was relying on me, and while I was frustrated and nervous, I was willing to do anything to ease her burden. So when he picked up the phone, I didn't beat around the bush.

"Hey bro, I need to tell you something . . ."

I could tell that Josh knew something wasn't right. At the time, we weren't the type of siblings to just call each other out of the blue.

"Uhh, okay..." he hesitantly replied.

Emotions clogged my throat and tears fell from my eyes as I said, "Mom was diagnosed with cancer."

There's something about saying those words that makes it all too real. I couldn't hide behind my innate strength or my role as the big sister. I think it was the first time that the full reality of the situation really hit me. Mom was sick, and not just a regular run-of-the-mill sick, but a life-threatening sickness that I could do absolutely nothing about. That was a major pain point for me. I had no control over anything that was happening. None of us did.

There was nothing but silence on the phone as he processed my words.

"Is she okay?" Josh asked.

"She's okay, but she will be starting chemo soon. And I'm going home to be with her for the first round," I said. "We need to be praying, and you should call her and talk to her."

I will forever be grateful for how my brother handled the news.

"Of course," he calmly replied. "God's got her, and I'll be praying. We'll all be okay." His reassurance was a balm to my soul.

"I'm gonna call her now," he said. "Love you, Jalesa."

"Love you, too, bro."

GAME PLAN

"What's the plan, Mom? Did the doctors say you need chemo?"

"Hey sweetie," she said, trying to sound as cheerful as possible. "Yeah, they said we have a solid plan moving ahead and chemo is part of it. First round starts next week."

"I'm coming home to be with you then," I swiftly replied.

I've always been the type to jump into action, even when I don't have all the answers. There's something about taking action that makes you feel as if you are in control. Even if you aren't. I was scared but ready to go to battle with Mom. So with a heavy heart but full of faith, I went to work the next day and informed my Navy leadership of my family emergency and within two weeks I arrived home to be with my mother for her first round of chemo.

Cancer is a scary battle to fight, not only for the patient but also for the loved ones who go on the journey with them. That's exactly what it is: a journey. It's an unexpected one that no one ever volunteers for, but many find themselves suddenly thrust into it. Just the word cancer sounds so final, but what I found is that if you give in to the fear then you're already admitting defeat. Our lives may have abruptly changed, but we were never the type of family to just throw in the towel. We had a game plan. Fight with everything we've got: medicine, faith, and love.

GETTING BATTLE-READY

One thing I learned while going through the cancer journey with my mother is that your mindset is half the battle. My mother was a warrior who was ready to fight, and her fighting spirit rallied up my spirit as well.

"Jalesa, I still got work to do!" she would proudly proclaim. "I have another thirty years at least."

Her words galvanized my faith. I believe the way we think says a lot about who we are, and once I learned of my mother's diagnosis, I knew that it was time to put on my big girl panties and be there for the woman who had always been there for me. Yes, there was hurt, pain, and frustration but in order for me to cope I couldn't allow myself to dwell on it.

Our minds are a constant battlefield. Like a ship at sea being tossed around in the middle of a storm, our minds can become overwhelmed with what life throws at us. It is a battle between the positive and negative. Between what is possible and what is not. Between the light and dark. Whatever thoughts dominate our minds has an effect on our behavior and even the outcome of our days sometimes.

I refused to think negatively about my mother's diagnosis. Despite the odds that were stacked against us, I wasn't going to quit the battle before it had even begun. On the days I felt overwhelmed and completely out of control, I turned to God. Sometimes I hid in my closet crying and praying to God for answers and listening to gospel music to both soothe and rejuvenate me. Although it was my mother's body being ravaged by cancer, I was determined to provide all the same love, positivity, and support that she provided me with my whole life. God had prepared me for such a time as this, and I answered the call to step up and be there for my mother.

QUESTIONS TO CONSIDER

How are you choosing to think about your circumstances?
Have you already given up, or are you going in battle-ready?

CHAPTER 2

CURVEBALLS OF LIFE

*What you're supposed to do when you
don't like a thing is change it.
If you can't change it, change the way
you think about it. Don't complain.*
*— Maya Angelou, Wouldn't Take Nothing
for My Journey Now*

In April 2019, I arrived at the Methodist Hospital in Memphis, Tennessee, with a determined mindset and bearing gifts for my mother. Before flying home, I did research on things to help my mother through her hospital stay. I went on Amazon buying things like lotion for cancer patients, tummy drops for nausea caused by chemo, a journal for her to document her journey, and even a blanket with encouraging words on themes of hope, faith, and love. No warrior goes into battle unprepared, and I was determined my mother would be more than prepared.

I can clearly remember the first time I walked into my mother's hospital room. I didn't know what to expect, but there she was fully dressed sitting on her hospital bed animatedly talking with her nurse.

"Look Jalesa, the chemo is purple!" Purple is my favorite color.

I was a little surprised because although there was an IV in her arm, everything about my mother seemed completely normal. When you get the news of a loved one being diagnosed with cancer, you look for the signs. Hair loss, weight loss, skin pigment discoloration. Looking for the worst. But cancer had yet to take a toll on her. Instead, it can move stealthily, giving you a false sense of "oh, it's not that bad." I couldn't fathom that cancer was really in her body. She looked as she always did and for me that gave me some comfort.

"This is my oldest, Jalesa," my mom excitedly introduced me to her nurse. "Yea, my baby flew in just to be with me for my first round of chemo," she gushed.

"Hi, nice to meet you," I said to her nurse.

"Your mother is a sweetheart," the nurse told me.

I wasn't surprised by her words. Most people instantly loved my mom when they met her.

"Hi, Mrs. Lowe!" A staff member joyfully called out to my mom as she entered the room with her lunch. "I brought you an extra chocolate pudding since I know you like those."

"Oh, thank you so much, dear heart," my mother replied sweetly.

There was so much joy in the room as nurses and staff members came in and out lingering to talk with my mom. *Okay, we can do this! Everything is going to be okay,* I thought as I watched my mom receive her chemo.

THE HIDDEN BATTLE

While my mother still physically looked the same, there was an internal battle that my mother and I were both fighting. She was a natural caretaker who loved to take people under her wings. She'd never met a stranger a day in her life and was always loving on people. I loved to invite my friends to my home when I was in high school, and she would encourage it. She was always asking them about their lives and listened intently as they shared their woes, or she would laugh and tease them lightheartedly about their latest crush. It was never a dull moment with her, and I was proud to share her with my friends. She exuded a type of warmth that people gravitated to without them even realizing it.

"Hi dear heart, how are you?" That was one of her favorite terms of endearment for people. She always had a smile and hug for anyone who needed it. But she didn't know how to let other people be there for her.

"Mom, who all know what's going on with you?" I asked her as I sat beside her while she laid in the hospital bed.

"I haven't told anyone."

I was flabbergasted. I couldn't believe that she was keeping her condition a secret!

"You need to tell at least our family and friends." I was frustrated thinking to myself, *How in the world will you get the support you need if no one knows?!*

She sat quietly, but I could tell that she was thinking about what I said. It was at this point that my dad came into the room, having gotten there right after work.

"Hey! How are my girls doing?" While the mood in

the room was dampened a little from our conversation, he brought in light, lifting our spirits.

Timothy stood at 6'4". In my eyes, my father has always been a giant, both in height and character. While I got my looks from my mother, I got my personality from him. Something that Mom always jokingly begrudged. My dad can be as serious as they come one minute and the life of the party the next. He was our strong tower during this journey.

When Dad came into the room, Mom started sobbing.

"What's going on?" he asked, looking at me, confused.

I explained to him that I was trying to understand why Mom wasn't letting family and friends know about her diagnosis.

"I don't know how!" she wailed.

My heart broke for her. While my mother knew how to be there for others, she didn't know how to let others be there for her.

"Oh honey, people love you," Dad said.

"Yea Mom, you have to give people a chance to be there for you. You don't have to tell everyone, but you need to start somewhere," I insisted.

My dad was in full agreement. By the end of our conversation, we convinced her to reach out to two of her closest friends—one of them being my godmother. And by the time I left to go back to Maryland, my godmother was visiting her in the hospital, which comforted me as I knew my mom was in caring hands.

I was a firm believer that it was time for her to cash in on all the love she had been giving out to others over the years.

DEALING WITH LIFE'S DISAPPOINTMENTS

I realize now that my mother may have been struggling with the disappointments she'd endured in her life. Christine Clark was the last child of Willie Mae Clark. She was the youngest of six, with one brother and four sisters, and the only child with a different father. She was an unexpected blessing that her mother loved fiercely, but she never felt fully accepted by her siblings, especially her sisters. And her biological father was never around in a permanent way.

Her whole life she struggled with wanting to be accepted by her sisters. While I believe in some ways she was accepted, there was always an underlying hurt of not being fully embraced by all of them.

In the case of her father, their relationship was a complicated one. My maternal grandfather was 60 years old when my mother was born. She was a surprise that he tried to have my grandmother abort, but after Mom was born, he changed his tune and constantly bragged about having a beautiful young daughter in his old age. Even so, her childhood was full of hurt and disappointment from him.

If her own blood couldn't give her the love and affection she needed, then how did she expect others to be there for her in her time of need?

Mom had had enough disappointments in her life, and she didn't want to give others the chance to hurt her.

While Mom struggled with letting others be there for her, I was struggling with anger towards my godsister.

Serenity was a sarcastic fourteen-year-old that came into my life when I was just four years old. She became a part of our family as if she was always there. Despite our ten-year difference, she never treated me as if I was a nuisance (even though I know I was). I loved her fiercely which is why it broke my heart when she suddenly disappeared from our lives.

"Meet my daughter, Jalesa. She came from Maryland to be with me for my first round of chemo." My mom was beaming as she talked with her nurse.

"I have two other kids. Joshua, my son, and my goddaughter Serenity." I grimaced at the mention of my godsister, but I tried to hide it from mom.

When the nurse left my mother asked, "What was that look?"

I tried to play stupid, but my mother was sharp as a tack. She wasn't fooled. "Why did you make that face when I mentioned Serenity?"

Dang it! Why can't I have a poker face?!

I remember the first time someone pointed out to me that I didn't hide my emotions very well.

My seventh-grade year, my mother enrolled me into a Catholic school. One day, a nun came into class lecturing us on our bad behavior. I was pulled from the classroom because of the face I made.

"Do you know what a poker face is?" the nun asked. I scrunched up my face as I answered, "No."

"Well, sweetie, you don't have one," she replied.

To this day that makes me laugh.

"You're still claiming her, even though she hasn't spoken to us in a year?" I asked my mom.

I was livid with Serenity. The previous year she had started ignoring all our calls and refused to call us back. She even missed my wedding. None of us knew why she'd cut us off. Underneath the anger I knew I was hurt, but I refused to acknowledge it.

"Yes, she's still a part of this family. I don't know what's going on with her, but I'm not disowning her," Mom said.

"Fine, then she needs to know what's going on with you," I said.

"No, I don't want to tell her."

"But Mom..."

"No, I want her to come back home because she wants to. Not because she feels obligated."

I was floored. I couldn't believe that my mother was choosing not to tell her. I was so angry with my sister, and although a part of me felt she didn't deserve to be there after cutting us off, I also felt that it was her duty to be there.

"You need to let go of your anger, Jalesa. She's still your sister, and I know you love her."

Throughout my mother's cancer journey, there would be many times when I would struggle with the decision of whether I should let my sister know what was going on or not. There were countless times when I would agonize over it with my husband. *What would I say? Should I just text her what is going on?* But I wanted to honor my mother's wish. And a big part of me didn't know if I could ever forgive

Serenity.

ADJUSTING TO LIFE

Life will throw you curveballs. God knows I've dealt with plenty in my life. After graduating from college and not being able to find a job in my field because I didn't have "enough work experience," I went home feeling like a failure as I moved back in with my parents. When life sets us on a new path, we need to adjust. Continuing as if nothing has changed does not serve you. You can't stick your head in the sand hoping that if you ignore your problems long enough, they will go away. We are not meant to live in fear of our circumstances. Instead, we must face them head-on, knowing that God has equipped us to handle all that life throws at us.

The curveball that life threw at my family in the form of cancer uncovered things that we needed to deal with. For my mother, it was trust issues that lingered. For me, it was letting go of anger and hurt caused by a close loved one.

QUESTIONS TO CONSIDER

What anger are you holding on to? What person or life circumstance has disappointed you most?
Who or what have you lost trust in?

Take a moment to acknowledge it. We can't let go of what we don't acknowledge.

CHAPTER 3

NEVER LOSING HOPE

For God has not given us a spirit of fear and timidity,
but of power, love, and self-discipline.
— 2 Timothy 1:7 (NLT)

As my family began to adjust to our new normal of my mother constantly visiting the hospital for checkups and taking all kinds of pills to assist in health, life continued. It's so true what they say: time waits for no one. My father still had to work and felt the pressure of balancing his work life and trying his best to be there for my mother. It was a constant struggle.

My mother would call me crying because she wanted him to be there for her at every appointment and tend to her needs, and while my father wanted to do that, he also needed to make sure that he made up for their income loss since she could no longer work. It was a battle into which my mother often pulled me. I tried my best to see both sides, but because I lived in another state, it was hard to understand what exactly was going on.

"Mom, this is why you need to let others be there for

you. Dad has to go to work."

"I know that, Jalesa, but I feel like he doesn't understand how much I need to feel his support right now. He's not being sensitive enough," she said.

"I'm sure he's doing his best to support you. You're both tired. He just needs to be able to get rest sometimes so he can give you his best. He's trying, Mom. I talked to him, and he just needs rest sometimes."

"Oh, so you've been talking to him, huh?"

I knew I slipped up by telling her that. From there, our conversation completely deteriorated, and as we abruptly ended our call, I was left feeling mad, hurt and confused.

You're not supposed to fight with your sick mother. But what do you do when the two people you love most are both coming from different perspectives, causing a bit of a rift at such a crucial time?

My mother and I had the kind of relationship that we didn't go more than two days without talking to each other. My junior year in college I would work late night shifts as a front desk attendant in my campus apartments. One night, at midnight, my roommate came bursting into the lobby yelling at me.

"Jalesa! Here you are!" I was shocked. "Girl, yo' momma been calling around trying to find you! Why aren't you answering your phone?!" My phone was dead, and I didn't have my charger. I couldn't help but laugh as I called my mom to assure her that I was fine. Because I wasn't answering my phone, she took it upon herself to call my roommate! That was us. We would go to the ends of the earth to find and communicate with each other.

You can only imagine how it pained me to not talk to

her when she was sick. I tried my best to communicate with her that Dad and I were doing our best to accommodate her, but Mom could be as stubborn as she was sweet when she put her mind to it. We ultimately agreed to disagree. In the grand scheme of things, we were all doing our best and this didn't stop us from loving each other wholeheartedly.

FINDING A NEW NORMAL

Amid my mother beginning her treatments, I was preparing to separate from the United States Navy. Despite the emotional stress of what was happening back home with my mom, I was excited to begin a new chapter in my life. I had managed to get an internship with a marketing company, and I was over the moon that I was finally working in the field I always dreamed about.

My mother was ecstatic for me as well. The first week of my internship I received a card in the mail from her that I proudly displayed on my desk at work.

6/2/19

Congratulations again on this new endeavor you are about to embark upon in your career. Remember, there's greatness inside of you. Don't ever doubt it. Don't ever sell yourself short and don't ever allow intimidation to stop you or cause you to question who God has created you to become.

Love Always,
Mom

It was such a contradicting time in my life. While I was

experiencing a career high, it was somewhat dampened by what was happening in my personal life. But I tried my best never to let it show.

Instead, I established a new normal. Every day I went to work ready to learn and give my best, and during my lunch breaks, I would call my mom to check in with her. We talked about anything and everything during those breaks. You see, my mom was more than just my mother, she was my best friend. I could always talk to her about anything, so that didn't change after her diagnosis, but our conversations would often be more serious. We talked about our dreams and the future, and most times we laughed about what was going on in our lives. Cancer may have been a part of our lives, but we refused to let it take over. Those conversations were some of the best I ever had with her.

Sometimes we would talk several times a day, and any time she didn't answer the phone, a bit of fear would sneak in and attack my heart. *"Is she okay? Why isn't she answering the phone?"*

My life now consisted of a constant underlying worry that I refused to acknowledge. When she would call back and leave a message, it was like a weight was lifted off my chest.

"Hey sugar! I saw where I missed a call from you earlier. Try to call me back no later than... 9, 9:15 'cause Imma be going down by then. Alright."

To this day, I still have that voicemail saved on my phone.

In some ways, my life had become unrecognizable. I was constantly checking for updates on my mom's health, worrying every time I got a phone call from home, and finding quiet places to cry. But it was my new normal and I learned to grin and bear it.

HOPE

In the early stages of my mother's journey, the doctors explained to us that the only real chance my mother had of achieving remission was a bone marrow transplant. The National Cancer Institute defines remission as "a decrease in or disappearance of signs and symptoms of cancer."

This was the miracle we needed. I put my hope in God first, but my hope in finding a donor was a close second.

"And if you can't find a donor, then what?" I asked the doctor. I had hope, but I was also a realist.

"Children are an automatic 50% match," the doctor replied. "We would ask your brother to donate his bone marrow. It would be better for your mother to get it

Did You Know?

A patient's ethnic background greatly affects the likelihood of someone finding a bone marrow match. On the Be The Match Registry®,
the likelihood ranges from 29% to 79% based on ethnic background.
Take a wild guess which ethnic group has the lowest percentage.
If you said African Americans,
then you would be right.

For more information and to consider being a donor, please check out **bethematch.org.**

from him than you. Females develop antibodies after giving birth that make it hard to receive a transplant from their own daughters."

On my first visit to see my mom in the hospital, her doctors laid out the plan to get my mother in remission. It was going to be a long battle and the chemo was just the first step.

I spent that first week of chemo with her sleeping in the uncomfortable chair next to her bed, watching movies, having conversations with the staff, and praying for a miracle. All while keeping up with my master's program assignments. When I went back to Maryland to continue my life, I made sure to keep up with the progress of my mother's condition.

"Is your white blood count down? Have they found a donor?" I asked my mom.

"They haven't found a donor with a high enough match, so your brother has agreed to come home and do it."

Thank God!

I was happy and hopeful that Josh's bone marrow would be the answer to our prayers.

KNOCKED DOWN, BUT NOT DESTROYED

After Mom received the transplant, it was a waiting game. We all lived life as normally as possible. Mom was no longer working, so when she wasn't resting or going for checkups, she would spend her days with Dad's mom or his sister. Dad continued to work, Josh went back to his base in Louisiana, and I started my next courses in my MBA program while continuing my internship. Life doesn't stop when it throws you a curveball, so we kept moving right along with it.

It was in October when I got the call.

While I was sitting at my desk at work, I got a text from my mom asking if I could talk. I went into a room alone to speak with her. As soon as I heard her voice, I knew something was wrong.

"The transplant didn't work."

My heart immediately dropped. This was the miracle we were counting on. The treatment that we were praying and hoping would work. With leukemia, there aren't a lot of options.

"So, what do we do now?" I asked her. "Do we have any other options?"

I held my tears back because I didn't want my mother to hear me cry. I always made sure to be strong for her and never let her hear my voice waver since the moment she first told me about her diagnosis. This time was no different.

I could hear in her voice that she was feeling a little defeated, but I refused to add to it.

"They will keep monitoring my white blood count, and they'll try to use the last of Josh's bone marrow that he donated."

Okay, this is good. We still have a chance.

It was a brief conversation. I prayed for her, and we got off the phone. As I sat alone in that room, I couldn't help but to give into the sadness I was feeling, if only for a moment. I allowed myself a few tears, found the strength to get up and went home to tend to my battered heart.

We had lost this battle, but I was determined we would win the war. My hope was still strong.

DON'T GIVE UP

My family had no clue how to deal with my mother's diagnosis. None of us had been close with anyone that had cancer. We were all feeling our way in the dark with nothing but a tiny candle to guide us.

Mom only wanted close family to be there for her. She felt that my dad wasn't sensitive enough to her needs and wanted him to spend more time with her.

On the other hand, my dad was trying to figure out how to be there for my mom and give her the best care possible, work more hours and take care of the house.

I was trying to figure out how to support my family from long distance, transition out of the military and keep up with getting my master's degree.

My brother was freshly new in the Air Force living in another state as well and figuring out his first serious relationship.

We had no clue what we were doing! But we did our best. There is no perfect answer for how to deal with cancer. Everyone reacts differently, but for us we simply clung to faith and despite our differences we made sure to always lead with love.

Psalm 119:105 says, "Your word is a lamp to guide my feet and a light for my path" (NLT). We took this Scripture to heart. Every step we took was guided by God. We were ignorant to how we should or should not act. We simply trusted in God and our love for each other.

So, if you're looking for a step-by-step guide on how to deal with cancer, I'm sorry to disappoint you, but this book isn't that. I just hope that by reading this, you'll learn from our interactions to lead with love and the never-failing faith and hope we tried our best to keep alive.

When is the last time you allowed yourself to feel hope?
Are you inspiring hope or instilling fear in your situation?

CHAPTER 4

THE LAST CHRISTMAS

Never succumb to the temptation of bitterness.
— Martin Luther King, Jr.

Mom continued with her checkups and taking the plethora of pills the doctors prescribed her. Meanwhile, I was lost on what to do. After Mom told me about the transplant not working, I could barely concentrate on my classes. I was already struggling with the workload, and with this news any chance of me passing my classes was shot. So, I made the decision to withdraw from my classes.

I didn't tell my mother because I didn't want her to worry. She was always proud of how well I did in academics, but at that point I could not care less about getting an MBA degree. However, I kept working. My internship was going well as we headed into the holidays, and there was a good chance they would hire me once my internship was complete.

To have everything going so well in one area but feeling like life was falling apart in another—my life held a jarring contrast.

"You should go home to see your mom." My cousin had called to check in with me.

"I'm going home in January for her birthday," I replied.

"No, you need to go sooner."

I didn't understand why my cousin was insisting that I go home. My mom was fine, or at least as fine as she could be with cancer ravaging her body. I'd been talking to her regularly, and despite the transplant not going well, things were at least stable with her. Besides, my mom was a pretty vocal person when it came to her wants and needs. If she wanted me home, she would have told me.

"You never know what could happen. It'll be good for you to go see her."

It was November, and I was almost done with my internship. Daniel and I had plans to go to Iceland for a friend's 30th birthday, which my mother knew about, and I was planning on going to see her right before that.

Ugh! Why is she pressing me like this?!

"I'll think about it, but I'll keep my plans to visit mom in January for now," I told my cousin.

I was in no rush to go home, and I was honestly quite frustrated with my cousin for rattling my reality. I didn't need any reminders that Mom was sick. She was "stable," and that is what I held on to. I wanted to live life as normally as possible—to enjoy it and not think about the fact that she could possibly slip through my fingers at any moment. I was content in knowing that Mom was okay. She wasn't in any immediate danger, so as far as I was concerned, everything was alright.

"Jalesa, I need you to come home." It was maybe just a couple weeks after talking to my cousin that my dad asked me to come home.

"What's going on, Dad? Is everything okay?" I asked. I was alarmed – my dad rarely asked for help with anything. From the outside looking in, he took every obstacle in stride and remained strong.

"Everything is okay, but I think it'll be good for your mom if you come home and spent time with her," he replied. Some may say this was a coincidence, but I knew it was a sign from God.

I have always strived to be a good daughter. I can be independent to a fault sometimes and stubborn, but when my parents really needed me, I always did my best to come through for them.

"Okay, Dad. I'll look for flights tonight and send you the details later."

Two weeks later, I was on a flight back home to see my mother.

A Sign from God

Mom had no idea I was coming to visit her. She still thought I was coming for her birthday. My 29th birthday had just passed, and she requested that I send her pictures from when I went out with my friends.

She texted: *I never knew that you would be a Fashionista! You are a force to be reckoned with!!*

Mom would always joke that when I was younger, I had no fashion sense. Thank God I grew out of that!

When I called her later that day, she gushed about the purse I was carrying in my pictures. "It's so cute! Can you get me one in the same color?" That same week I went out and bought her the purse.

I went home the week before Christmas, so I came bearing gifts, including the purse.

"Hey Dad, I just landed. I'm going home first to drop my things off then heading to the hospital."

"Great! Thank you for coming home, Jalesa. She's gonna be so excited to see you." I could hear the smile on my dad's face.

I called my mother after getting to the house to make sure she wasn't sleeping.

"Hey ma, how you doing this morning?"

"Hi dear heart, I'm doing okay. Just got done having some quiet time this morning. What are you doing?"

"Oh, I'm working from home today. I just wanted to call and check on you." As I got off the phone with mom, I was eager to get to the hospital and surprise her.

Just 40 minutes later, I was knocking on her hospital door.

"Hello…" I called out as I opened the door. "Hi there!" I exclaimed as I saw Mom's face.

I recall the look of pure shock on her face.

"How you doing…why you looking at me like that?" I asked, laughing at her expression. "How you doing there?"

Mom laid back on her bed, closed her eyes and smiled.

"Christmas came early!" I exclaimed.

"Give me a minute. Just give me a minute," she softly said.

"I'm going home!" she suddenly said.

"You going?!" I laughed.

"Yea, I ain't staying here. I'm going home," she proclaimed as she reached for a hug.

"What you mean you going home? You can't go home till the people tell you to go home," I jokingly reminded her.

Christmas had come early, and she refused to spend her time in the hospital while I was home.

Seeing her this time was a shock to the system. Although I'd seen her on our many video calls and she'd sent me pictures, it was still a shock to see her with no hair, and her skin complexion was darker. She didn't look as lively this time, but still had some of her spark.

Honestly, it felt good to hug her, and I knew in that moment I did the right thing by coming home. As I sat and I talked with my mother, I was awed by her strength and vulnerability.

The time she spent in the hospital gave her time to think and pray about things she'd never dealt with before. She cried to me as she spoke about wanting to feel the love of a father. She'd never really had a true relationship with her dad, so she relied heavily on God.

"Sometimes, I wish I could just reach up and get a hug from God," she cried.

My heart broke for my mother. We sat in that hospital bed crying and laughing together. It would be months after she passed that my dad would find a recording of my mother on her phone. She didn't understand why it had to be her to go through this trial, but she was still hopeful that God would come through for her: "I just need one sign, God, that this will be over soon and very soon."

When I heard her words on that recording, I completely broke down in tears. The recording was from the same day I came home and surprised my mother. While we were sitting in that bed crying and laughing, Mom looked at me and said, "I asked God for a sign." It wouldn't be until after she passed that I realized she was telling me that I was her sign.

The day after I arrived, Mom was released from the hospital, and we went home. That week before Christmas was filled with joy. I didn't know then it would be my last holiday with her, but I'm so grateful for that last Christmas with her.

BEING BITTER

You may be thinking, *Aren't you bitter or mad at God?*

The simple answer is no.

The honest answer is a bit more complicated than that.

Mom asked for a sign from God that everything would be alright. She wanted a miracle. We all wanted and prayed for a miracle. I think sometimes we ask God for things, but He answers how He sees fit.

I thought about being bitter or mad. At first, I told myself there was no point in being upset. God knows and sees things we can't possibly understand, so who am I to question Him? But as time has gone on, I realized that there is an underlying hurt that I'm still working to resolve.

Whenever I hear a story of someone being miraculously healed, there is a part of me that retreats within myself. I ask myself why that couldn't be my mom's story. The raw truth is I wonder what's so special about those other people that God saw fit to save them. But then I feel terrible for having those thoughts because I know that we are all special in God's eyes. No one is more or less deserving of life than anyone else.

This is why I don't let myself go down that line of thinking for too long. One thing I learned from Mom while she battled leukemia is that it is a waste of time to be angry and rage at God. Instead, we must use our time wisely and learn the lessons that God is teaching us.

I've had plenty of time to think about this. She asked for a sign and believed that I was it. I would love nothing more if she were still here, but I choose to believe that when she asked for that sign and saw me, it was God's way of telling her that the future would be taken care of through her children.

I could be reaching for an explanation, but it's the only thing that makes sense to me.

We never understand the ways of God. His thinking is far beyond ours, but my mother chose to trust Him her whole life, even more during her cancer battle, and I choose to do the same now.

QUESTIONS TO CONSIDER

Are you bitter with God? What about your situation makes you the angriest?

It's okay if you are. God can handle our bitterness and anger. We wouldn't be human if we didn't feel those things.

What are your frustrations?

Write them out and present them to God. I promise He won't be offended.

CHAPTER 5

BEGINNING OF THE END

Love is patient and kind...
— 1 Corinthians 13: 4 (NLT)

January 2020

I was no longer in the military and had successfully made the transition into a job role with the marketing company. Things were looking up for me.

Hey Jalesa, just calling to let you know that they are going to readmit me to the hospital. The head congestion that I have has made its way down to my chest and I have some wheezing so they're going to get on top of it right away. Just wanted to let you know.

She sounded awful on the phone. She could barely speak, and she coughed like she was hacking up a lung. I was terrified.

"Dad, is Mom okay? She doesn't sound good."

"She has a pretty bad cold, but we're taking care of it," he replied.

Mom ended up spending her birthday in the hospital, and soon after she started asking me to come home again.

"I was just there, Mom. Plus, me and Daniel have

that to trip to Iceland, remember? I can't keep leaving work."

"I know, but I really want you here," she said.

Shamefully, when I look back on this time, I was getting frustrated with my mom. I didn't understand then that she needed me. But frustrated or not, I never wanted to displease her.

"When we get back from Iceland, I'll see what I can do."

Later that month my husband and I visited Iceland for a friend's birthday. Some would say that going out of the country while your mom is sick is risky and insensitive, but I needed this trip. My life was full of stress and worry, and I just wanted something for myself to enjoy. Iceland turned out to be a beautiful place that I didn't expect to love. From the snowy mountains, icy glaciers and choppy seas, Daniel and I fell in love with Iceland. Thankfully, my parents supported us taking the trip.

By this time, she had been back in the hospital for a couple weeks. I made sure to call my parents and text pictures of our adventures.

Me: *We're here and already enjoying ourselves!*

Dad: *Awesome!! Praying that you both have the time of your lives!!!*

Mom: *Gorgeous sceneries*

I bought gifts for Mom, knowing that she would be appalled if I didn't. Mom was like that. She loved when someone thought enough of her to buy something thoughtful (mainly her children), and it was because she was always thinking of others.

However, when we got back from Iceland, there was a breakdown in communication with my mother that I regret to this day. She was asking me to come home more and more, and in my immaturity, I started avoiding some of her calls.

Mom texted me: *Hello, I miss hearing from you. Are you alright?*

When I called her, the guilt hit me full-force immediately.

"Jalesa, I need you. You're my kingdom warrior, and I rely on you. Even if you can't call, at least send a text message," Mom said.

This is something that will always tear at my heart. The fact that Mom had to ask me to be there for her—I'm not sure if I'll ever get over that aching regret.

February 2020

I finally went home for a week in February.

Mom was getting worse, and I was getting more frustrated. She was...different. There was no spark in her eye anymore. She barely had the strength to get up and walk. She wasn't eating enough food, and she could barely stay awake to hold a conversation.

I was starting to get scared, and the only way I knew how to express it was through encouragement and poorly restrained frustration and anger.

"Mom, you have to get up and walk. You need to exercise at least once a day."

"I'm tired right now. I'll take a walk later."

All she does is sleep! She asked me to come here, and she doesn't even talk to me. Just sleeps!

I was getting angry. I spent that week with her having short conversations in between her naps, trying to get her to eat and exercise, and helping her shower. It was a struggle. This visit was different from the others, and I was so blinded by frustration that I was missing all the signs.

"Daniel, she's not even trying!" I cried to my husband over the phone. I had snuck out of Mom's room while she was taking one of her naps. I paced back and forth in the hospital lobby as I expressed my anger and fear.

"I think she's trying to give up! I'm so angry with her. She asked me to come here, and she's not even trying!" He listened to me as I ranted and cried, and waited for me to calm down.

"Babe, I understand you're upset, but you just need to be there for her," my husband spoke calmly.

He was right of course, but it didn't stop the frustration from festering in my heart. However, I dried my tears and headed back into battle (her room), ready to fight some more.

"I want to go home," Mom said the next day.

"Mom, you can't go home. You have to stay here." Mom was still dealing with the cold she had caught (which I now believe may have been COVID-19), and the doctors were trying to convince her to do another round of chemo.

"I just want to go home for like a day. I just want to sit on my couch," she said with some sadness.

I let my dad know that Mom was talking about going home. I was scared to let her go home. She was in no condition to leave the hospital. And the doctors were hinting at hospice if she went home.

"Well, maybe it would be good for her to go home," my aunt said over the phone. My dad's youngest sister called me after he told her what Mom had said. I must confess that

I was stubborn.

"It may do her some good to go home," my aunt repeated. But I didn't want to listen. I needed Mom to stay in the hospital so she could get better. Ultimately, I discouraged Mom from going home because I couldn't see past the fact that she was sick. I admit now that I was also scared that once she got home, we wouldn't be able to get her to go back to the hospital, which would mean certain death for her. Mom going home felt like admitting defeat, and I couldn't handle that.

A Glimpse of Love

I was always fascinated with how well my dad took care of Mom. Where I would get frustrated, he took his time with her. Mom not walking was really upsetting me, so one evening when Dad got to the hospital after work, he tried his best to gently encourage her to walk.

Mom wasn't having it! She had managed to get out of bed and sit in a chair, and that was as far as she was going to go.

"Christine," my dad called softly when he entered the room. "Let's go for a walk, honey." Mom sat peacefully in the chair with her eyes closed and shook her head no.

"Babe, c'mon now. You know you need to get your exercise in," he continued. He began to gently try to pull her out of the chair. Suddenly, mom's eyes flew open wide, and clear as a bell she said, "I said no, Tim." It was the strongest I'd heard her voice in a while. Dad just laughed it off, and I was in awe as we both realized that while she may be physically weak, she was still sharp as a tack in her mind. It was good to know she still had some of her bite.

Dad knew when Mom was serious. She wasn't going for a walk, so instead he helped her get back into bed. But before she got in bed, she held on to him as tightly as she could as he hugged her. I watched as my parents had a quiet moment that shouted support and love. I couldn't help but to get a picture. They were the very picture of "through sickness and health."

SWEET DREAMS

I got Mom to take a walk one time during the week that I was there. What should have been a five-minute walk turned out to be more like 15 minutes, but I didn't care. I was just glad that I finally convinced her to get out of the bed. We started our leisurely walk—her walking painstakingly slow as I rolled her IV next to her. As we made our way down the hall, one of the nurses stopped to talk with Mom.

"How are your kids doing?" Mom asked the nurse. "I haven't seen you in a while." The nurse smiled brightly as she told Mom that she and her kids were doing well. I was in awe at how my mother took the time to stop and ask about someone. She was clearly tired and weak, and it took a lot out of her just to have a conversation, but that was the epitome of who my mother was. A humble woman who took the time to care for others in the smallest ways even when she was in pain.

As we continued to walk with me holding her hand, I was even more aware of how precious and fragile she was.

"I had a dream," Mom suddenly said. "It was a baby boy." My heart leaped in my chest. I've always wanted a little boy.

"He was a little light-skinned baby and so cute and happy," she said.

"Oh yea? You dreaming about your future grand-child, Mom?" I jokingly asked.

She just gently smiled as we continued to walk. I took my mother's dreams seriously because they always seemed to have special meaning. I was a little hopeful that night as we made our way slowly back to her room.

To this day I like to think that God was giving her a tiny glimpse of the future she wouldn't be able to be a part of.

This time when I went back home, I left feeling not as confident about Mom's condition.

WHAT DOES IT MEAN TO BE SELFLESS?

When dealing with a loved one who has cancer, it's a con-stant battle of what you should or shouldn't do. You want your loved one to get better, so of course you're going to do everything you can to make sure that happens, even if that means going against what they want. But when does looking out for them become more about you?

Looking back, I was selfish in some ways. When she asked me to come home again, I didn't want to go. I selfishly wanted to stay in Maryland so I could continue to work my job. And when I did go to visit her, I immaturely tried to push her to do more than she could handle.

I wanted her to get better. I wanted her to fight. I wanted her to do what she had to do so that she could walk out of that hospital cured.

It was no longer about her. I made it about me.

If you find yourself in a similar situation with a loved one, I encourage you to give them what they want if it's manageable. I lost sight of the fact that my mother was still a person who wanted to enjoy life but couldn't because cancer had robbed her of that. I can only imagine the frustration and sadness my mother experienced at not being able to do the simple things she enjoyed. So, learn from my mistakes and let your person experience all the little joys that they're able to. God calls us to put others before ourselves. As Paul so aptly put it: "Do nothing from selfish ambition or conceit, but in humility count others more significant than yourselves" (Philippians 2:3, ESV). When we do that, we are beyond blessed.

QUESTIONS TO CONSIDER

I think a part of me knew that things had taken a turn for the worse, but I didn't want to admit it.

What problems are you avoiding?

Who are you taking your frustrations out on?

CHAPTER 6

CALLING THE CAVALRY

I will send out an army to find you
In the middle of the darkest night
It's true, I will rescue you
— Lauren Daigle, "Rescue"

Nothing was normal when I went back home to Maryland. I was constantly worried about Mom. I called and sent messages, but she wasn't responding.

Good morning, Mom! Just thinking about you. I pray you have a good and blessed day. And remember to eat some food and keep up your strength!

"She's sleeping right now, Jalesa," Dad told me, for what felt like the hundredth time. Mom was always sleeping. And anytime she did answer the phone, she sounded tired and distracted. I was driving myself crazy trying to think of ways to keep her motivated. I could tell she was starting to let go, and I refused to let her do that.

Every time the phone rang, and I saw my dad's name on the screen, my heart would stutter. *Is this it? Is this the call when he tells me she's gone?*

I was slowly spiraling, but I was determined to hang on for her. If she didn't want to fight anymore, then I would.

LETTING GO

In early March I got a call on an early Saturday morning. My heart dropped.

"Hey Dad. What's going on?"

"Hey Jalesa." My dad's voice sounded a little weird. My heart started pounding fast.

"I just talked to your mom," he said slowly. *Oh, thank God!*

"She says she wants to be let go." My relief was short-lived. This was it. She was really giving up.

"Well, what are the doctors saying?" I asked. "Is there something else we can do? Another round of chemo?"

I sat in the bed next to my sleeping husband as I listened to my dad and tried my best to hold back tears.

"They're saying the only thing they can do is chemo or send her home," my dad explained. *She can't go home! She'll die!* My mind was in an utter panic.

"I'll talk to her about it, but I don't think she wants to do any more chemo." I could hear the tiredness in my dad's voice. "I think it's time to have your brother come home. I'm going to see if he can come back early from his deployment." My dad's voice was like a buzzing in my ear as I zoned out. I was drowning in feelings.

"Yea, you do that," I replied, dazed. I was hanging on by a thread.

I hung up the phone and burst into tears. My husband woke up in a panic not knowing what was going on. I sobbed as I explained to him what my dad told me.

"I have to go home, Daniel," I cried. "I can't let her go! I need you to go with me this time." As Daniel held me, we made plans to head back to Memphis.

HOPE REKINDLED

It was March 2020. The start of shutdowns across the world had begun, and my husband had to receive special permission to take leave. Fortunately, my brother was able to end his deployment early and get a flight from the Middle East. My heart was somewhat at ease because now Dad had someone with him to help encourage Mom.

While Daniel waited to hear from his leadership about his emergency leave request, I received good news from Dad.

"She decided to do another round of chemo!" my dad exclaimed over the phone. I was happily relieved.

"What happened? Did you talk to her?" I asked.

"No, Howard visited her while he was in town and talked to her about listening to her doctors and taking their advice," Dad said.

Howard is my cousin who is a Master Chief in the Navy. He and my mom grew up together. Although he was her nephew, they were less than ten years apart and treated each other more like brother and sister. If there was anyone who could convince my mother to continue with treatment besides my father and me, it was Howard.

I had hope again.

"Do you think it's time to call Serenity?" Dad asked me.

My godsister was still a sore subject for me, but I never considered myself to be a cruel person. I knew deep down that Mom would want her there even if she didn't voice it.

"Yea, I'll do it," I reluctantly told Dad. He already had enough on his plate. My brother Josh had safely made it back to Memphis from his deployment, and they were taking turns staying with Mom in the hospital. On top of that, Dad was still going to work.

"I tried calling her already, but she hasn't answered," Dad informed me.

I wasn't surprised. She hadn't answered our calls in almost two years. I had given up calling her way before Mom got sick.

I tried calling and texting but to no avail.

Hey Serenity. I know it's been a while. I have something important to tell you. Please call back.

I was running out of patience, and I knew that time was of the essence. Mom *needed* us, and I was going to do everything I could to make sure we were all there for her. She was always there for us in our time of need. Now, it was our turn to be there for her.

I hated people being in our business, but Serenity needed to know so I reached out to a mutual friend on Facebook.

Hey Katy. I have a favor to ask if you don't mind. Could you call me when you get a chance?

Within the hour, she called.

"When was the last time you talked to Serenity?" I asked. I got straight to the point when I got on the phone.

As I spoke with Katy, I let her know what had transpired over the last two years: from not hearing back from Serenity in almost two years, to my mother's diagnosis, and the battle we had been fighting for almost a year.

She was in shock to say the least, but she promised that she would reach out to my sister and let her know what was going on. I wasn't sure what to expect, but I had faith that things would work out.

Less than 30 minutes later, I received a call from Serenity. "Jalesa, what's going on? I tried calling Dad back, but he didn't answer."

It was a shock to hear her voice after so long. I had so many questions, and though there was a quiet hurt that lived inside of me, I pushed it all aside for Mom.

No one likes being the bearer of bad news, but Mom needed us, and I would do what needed to be done to make sure Mom knew she had everyone fighting for her.

"Mom has cancer. It's been almost a year," I stoically explained. Just as I began to tell her what was going on, she got a call from Dad. I was relieved that I didn't have to continue. I got off the phone with her to let Dad finish telling her the rest.

Everything was coming together. Daniel had received his approval to travel with me. The caveat was no flying, so we prepared to drive 15 hours in one day. Serenity also got her approval from the Navy as well, and she began her 25-hour trek from California to Tennessee.

"Mom, you have to be strong and hang in there. I'm on my way," I told her over the phone. Joshua spent a lot of his time by our mother's side when he got back from his deployment. Mom wasn't talking much anymore, so I asked him to put me on speaker phone so she could hear my voice. I wanted to make sure she knew that her kingdom warrior was on the way.

HOME

My husband and I drove into Memphis late on a Tuesday night. Serenity had made it home just an hour before us. The reason we were back home wasn't ideal, but it felt good to be in my childhood home with my family. We planned to visit Mom immediately the next day. With the rise of COVID-19, the hospital was only allowing two people to visit at a time so we decided that my sister and I would be the ones to go.

That next morning as we headed to the hospital, I was full of nervous energy. I wasn't sure what to expect, but I was ready. This visit was unlike all the visits before. As I walked into Mom's room, it was like an out of body experience. Mom was curled up on her side, looking small and fragile. There was a breathing tube in her nose to help her breathe, and she was sound asleep.

My heart stuttered in my chest at the sight, but I walked quietly and confidently into the room as Serenity followed me in.

"Mom?" I called out. Serenity wacked my arm warning me not to be too loud, but I was in my domain. This wasn't my first rodeo, and I was itching to hear Mom's voice.

"Mom, it's me. I'm here." I waited patiently as she slowly opened her eyes. She looked confused for a second, but when her eyes focused in on me, I could see tears welling up in her eyes.

"What took you so long?" she wailed. My heart broke at that question. But I smiled gently as I crouched down by her bedside and wiped her tears.

"I tried. I really tried," she said weakly, as tears slipped down her cheek.

"I know, Mom. It's okay. Don't cry," I whispered to her calmly.

As I reassured her that everything was okay, Mom settled down and a sense of peace seemed to quickly lull her back to sleep. Little did I know that it would be the last time I would ever hear her voice.

KNOWING WHEN TO LET GO

The Merriam-Webster dictionary defines hope as "a desire accompanied by expectation of or belief in fulfillment." Hope can be a tricky thing, because when do you cross the line from hope to denial?

The Bible tells us in Hebrews 11:1, "To have faith is to be sure of the things we hope for, to be certain of the things we cannot see" (GNT). My faith was strong, and I was hopeful that Mom would recover. I was so hopeful that I missed all the signs, or I just ignored them.

How do you know when you're about to lose a loved one? No one ever wants to admit defeat, and when it comes to death, I think we stick our heads in the sand. I was so determined to fight for my mom that I blew right past the signs. Maybe it was my coping mechanism that was kicking in, but I would encourage you to pay attention and watch for the signs. They're always there if we let ourselves see them.

Questions to Consider

Who's in your corner? Your family? Friends? Identify those you can rely on. There's strength in numbers. Never fight a battle alone.

Feel like you don't have anyone to rely on? I encourage you to find a counseling group in your community. Start your search with churches. You don't have to be a member or Christian to attend a group.

CHAPTER 7

THE END IS NEAR

Peace holds me when I'm broken,
Sweet peace that passes understanding.
When the whole wide world is crashing down,
I fall to my knees and breathe in Your peace.
— Ed Cash, "Peace," by Bethel Music

I was oblivious. Or maybe it was just denial. Either way, I didn't recognize the signs for what they were. My last week with Mom was beautiful and painful. In only the way she could, she brought all of us together. We each took turns staying with her in her hospital room. She was never alone.

The night I stayed with her, I held her hand for most of the night. Dad was supposed to stay with Mom that night, but as I got up to leave, Mom squeezed my hand as tightly as she could. That was her way of communicating. Mom could no longer talk. She had been transitioned from a breathing tube to a breathing mask. Without the mask she struggled to breathe.

I had spent most of the day with Mom in the hospital, and I was so tired, but Mom refused to let go of my hand as

I tried to say goodbye.

"Mom, I'll be back in the morning," I told her gently. She continued to squeeze my hand. "You don't want me to go?" She answered by squeezing my hand with all her might.

At that point, Mom didn't have a lot of lucid moments. She spent most of her time resting, so when she was awake it was so good just to look into her eyes, even if she couldn't talk.

She reached for a pen and paper and tried her best to write. Mom had some of the most beautiful handwriting, but this sickness had robbed her of even that. I held back tears as I tried my best to decipher what she was writing. Dad had come to relieve Serenity and me, and we all tried to figure out what message she was trying to give us. I could tell Mom was getting frustrated, but she kept trying. Finally, I realized that she was writing our names.

"Honey, do you want us all here?" Dad asked her. Mom gave a slight nod and stopped her struggle in writing now that she had gotten her message across to us. My brother was the only one missing in the room. We called him to see if he could get a ride to the hospital, but he couldn't make it that night.

Although I was tired, I held on to Mom's hand as Serenity left and Dad took a seat in the corner. She wanted me to stay, and I wouldn't let her down when she needed me.

That night my father and I kept watch over Mom, a late-night vigil. I barely got any sleep. Every time she shifted in bed it startled me awake. When the peaceful Christian music we were playing would come to an end, I would start it over again. At one point, she indicated that her stomach was bothering her and would squeeze my hand every time the pain was too much for her. I would gently rub her stomach in hopes that it would bring her some comfort. I was sore, hungry, and tired, but nothing could have kept me from watching and praying over her that night. The following day I went home and slept the whole day.

Halfway through our week-long visit, the hospital shut down. Cases of COVID-19 were running rampant, and the hospital took precautions to keep the staff and patients safe. Families couldn't visit their loved ones, but for those patients that were considered critical, visitors were still allowed.

Mom was considered critical.

I think either I was an idiot or God was protecting me from the obvious. All the signs were there, but I was operating on sheer faith by this point. It never occurred to me that she wouldn't make it.

After taking a day to recuperate from the night I spent with Mom, I went back to visit her. This time it was me, Dad, and Josh in the room. The previous night Serenity stayed with Mom and now Josh was taking over the vigil again.

Daniel and I had one full day left before heading back for Maryland. The plan was to go home, get a good night's rest and return in the morning to spend my last day with Mom.

That night I was hopeful as we stood around Mom's bed. I kept hearing the word "survivor." I knew it was God trying to tell me something. I interpreted it as God letting me know that Mom was going to survive her condition.

Shamefully, I stayed half hidden behind Dad as we prepared to leave the room. I didn't want Mom to notice I was leaving. I thought she may try to get me to stay with her again, but before leaving her room I grabbed her hand as I spoke with full confidence.

"Mom, you're a survivor. You're so strong and you've had to survive all kinds of things. I keep hearing God say 'survivor,' and I believe that you're going to survive this," I declared.

I was so sure of my declaration.

As Dad and I left, Dad instructed Josh to call him if he needed anything. Dad and I walked down the halls of the hospital jubilantly as we praised God in advance for the miracle we were expecting.

"Mom's got this," I said joyfully.

"Christine is stronger than she thinks she is," Dad agreed.

Our joy and laughter were palpable.

Looking back, sometimes I wish I'd stayed in that room.

PEACE BEFORE THE STORM

I couldn't fall asleep. It was late when we got home. Everyone was in bed. My husband slept beside me, but sleep evaded me.

For some reason, I was anxious. And I couldn't figure out why.

Have you ever experienced such an anxiousness that keeps you up at night? Since the time Mom was first diagnosed, I'd had many nights when I couldn't fall asleep. I had faith, but there was something about this night that was keeping me awake.

It was a little after one in the morning when I heard

Dad answer his phone. My heart thudded in my chest as I lie still in bed straining to hear his voice. I couldn't hear what he was saying, but a short time later I heard him moving around. I peeked my head out of the bedroom just when Dad opened his door, fully dressed.

"Who was that?" I asked.

"It was Josh. I'm going back up to the hospital," he said, hurriedly.

"Should I come too?" My heart was beating a mile a minute.

"That's up to you," he said. "But I'm going down there now."

As Dad rushed out, I went upstairs to tell Serenity.

"What's going on?" she asked.

"Dad is going up to the hospital. I'm not sure what's going on," I said. I was beyond nervous. "Do you think we should go?" I asked her.

"If something happens, Dad will call," Serenity assured me. She had just spent the previous night with Mom, so I understood that she was tired.

As I climbed back into bed with Daniel, he lovingly soothed me.

"It's okay, babe. Just try and get some rest," he said. "You'll see her tomorrow."

My mind was on high alert, and I wasn't sure what to think, but right before drifting off to sleep while listening to Bethel's Peace album, I felt a sense of calm wash over me.

Everything was going to be okay.

Your Presence Is Needed

If I could have done more for my mother while she was in the hospital, there's no doubt I would have done it. But I've found that what helps in most cases like these is your presence. *Being there* is what counts the most. I try not to have regrets when I think back over the last year with my mom, but I can't help but think that I should have spent more time with her. All she wanted was for her family to be with her as much as possible.

The ideal situation would have been to quit my job and temporarily move back home to take care of my mother. But life's demands give absolutely no breaks, so we find ourselves trying to juggle several balls. In my case, I was juggling being a veteran, working a new job, trying to be a good wife, an impending move, and a sick mother who wanted me home. I didn't know how to manage, and in my immaturity, I believe that I missed parts of the bigger picture.

Calls and texts cannot replace showing up for your loved one in person. We all have excuses for why we can't be there, and sometimes they're *really good* excuses. But when you look back, those excuses mean nothing in the grand scheme of things. So be there. Show up for the people in your life. Life is too short to have regrets.

Questions to Consider

Who needs you right now?

What can you temporarily take off your plate to show up for the people in your life?

CHAPTER 8
FAREWELL

Smile, though your heart is aching
Smile, even though it's breaking
When there are clouds in the sky, you'll get by
— Nat Cole, "Smile"

Nothing was okay.

It was a little after seven in the morning when I woke up. I was surprised that I managed to get any sleep.

I checked my phone, but there were no calls or texts from Dad. I called his phone, but there was no answer.

How do you know when it's the end? Does anybody ever really know? No one is prepared for the end, even when it's obvious.

I remember clearly when my mom got the news that her mother passed. I was seventeen years old, just graduated from high school with no care in the world. It was late at night, and I was on the phone with my high school boyfriend. I barely paid attention to the house phone ringing in the distance.

Suddenly, a long piercing wail sounded throughout the house. It was like the sound of a dying animal. I dropped my phone and ran to find my mother broken down in tears. We all knew the end was near for grandma, but that didn't stop my mother's pain. While I watched her grieve and struggle with panic attacks, my teenage mind couldn't comprehend what she was feeling. I hurt for her and tried my best to comfort her when she needed it, but if I'm honest, my mind was preoccupied with my upcoming freshmen year in college. I was excited to get away from home and discover myself without adult supervision. Looking back on that time, I now realize how hard it must have been for my mom to lose her mother and then, in a way, lose me shortly after.

No one is ever prepared for the end, whether you see it coming or not.

Mom's death blindsided me...

Dad finally called me back after I called him a couple times.

"Jalesa, your mom is gone."

Those five words obliterated my world in a way I never expected. It was like the air was knocked out of my lungs as I tried to understand what Dad had just told me on the phone. My mother, my confidante and best friend, was no longer living.

"But I just saw her last night." "This can't be real!" "What am I gonna do?" "Why, God?" My thoughts were like jagged pieces that ripped through my mind as I began to sob.

Christine Clark Lowe passed peacefully with her husband and son at her side in the early morning on March 24, 2020.

The ground was ripped out from under me, and I was falling into a void.

Visceral pain. Utter panic. Disbelief.

It felt as if a fist was crushing my heart.

I don't remember what I said. There was crying. I was coherent enough to tell Daniel and Serenity, and after that my mind was blank.

STRENGTH

Mom looked peaceful, lying in her hospital bed. It was as if she was asleep, but when I bent to kiss her cheek, her cold skin let me know that her spirit was no longer in this world.

Daniel, Serenity and I had rushed to the hospital so we could see Mom before they took her body. The only sounds in the room were sniffles as we said our goodbyes, gathered her things and left the hospital.

Our next stop... the funeral home.

Somewhere between Dad telling me the news, going to see Mom's body, and driving to the funeral home, I had made up my mind that I was going to be the strong one.

As the oldest biological child, I felt it was my duty to hold the family together. While it was devastating that I had lost my mother, I couldn't help but think of the turmoil Dad must be going through after losing his wife of 32 years.

I was determined to get us through the process of planning Mom's funeral.

A COVID FUNERAL

Here's the thing about planning a funeral...no one warns you of how jarring the experience is. You've just lost a loved one, and now you're expected to plan their funeral in the same week! But planning a funeral at the beginning of COVID? That was another level of difficult.

Funeral homes were limiting the number of mourners that could be in a room, churches were shut down and no one could ride in the hearse. What was already a difficult time in our lives felt almost impossible during that time.

Because it was my first time experiencing such a personal loss, I was not aware of how fast paced it was to plan a funeral.

Less than an hour after leaving the hospital, we were sitting in a funeral home, being shown caskets. Dad was at a loss for words. As we sat there in that room, shell-shocked from our loss, I took it upon myself to make calls, order flowers and inform our loved ones of Mom's passing. There is no best practice to process something as jarring as planning a funeral for a loved one, especially minutes after the loss. I simply took one step at a time as we planned to bury my mother.

That same day we had to decide if we wanted Mom to be interred, entombed, or cremated. I didn't even know there were more than two options! It was a cold and rainy day as we walked around the memorial park trying to decide what to do. We all thought carefully as we discussed what she would have wanted. *Would she want to be cremated? How did we feel about putting her in a tomb?* The questions were never ending. Ultimately, we decided to bury her in the "Garden of Grace."

The task of what clothes Mom would be buried in was left to me and Serenity. We chose the dress that she wore to my wedding. We went shopping for a shawl to match the dress, picked her jewelry, chose the wig she would wear, and decided the color her nails should be painted. To date, this is the most bizarre thing I've ever experienced.

None of us came prepared for a funeral, so we had to go shopping for clothes for the wake and service.

Everything was a whirlwind.

I didn't give myself a lot of opportunities to cry, but as we planned Mom's funeral, we stayed up late each night reminiscing and going through old pictures. In a way, it was cathartic.

Only by God's grace were we able to pull together a funeral in four days during a pandemic.

An old elementary friend of Mom's allowed us to have her funeral at his church. We were blessed to be able to have a social-distanced service with more than ten people. One of Mom's best friends sang at the service. And for those who didn't make it due to the pandemic, they made sure to show their love and support the best way they knew how.

It was a difficult time, but it was also a beautiful time. I had never been more aware of God's love and comfort than during that time.

THE EULOGY

We had two people drop out on giving the eulogy for the service. COVID-19 was scary. People were dying and no one wanted to be next or potentially be the reason their loved ones got sick. Seeing as we had just lost the matriarch of our family, we understood the precautions people were taking. So, when the two people we asked to deliver the eulogy decided to step back due to health reasons, the task fell to us.

As a family, Dad, Joshua, Serenity and I decided

each to contribute to the eulogy. I believe Mom would have wanted it that way. Who best to talk about her life than those who loved her most and who she loved most in the world?

Reflections of Love

Dad:

I'm just so grateful to God, and I could not walk in here and be sad because God has just been so good to us...as we began to reminisce on all the things God has allowed us to be able to do. The places we've been, the fun we've had, the things that we have done is just amazing...

I believe that in her heart and in her soul, she would just simply say, "It is well with my soul"... and that is just what I believe my wife would have said....

I've learned so many things from my wife, but the one thing that stands out the most is love. Christine C. Lowe taught me how to love and to love much. She taught me what it means to love in every sense of the word.

The Bible says that God is love, and Christine Lowe was the epitome of love. God gave her the gift of love.

Additionally, the Bible says that love covers a multitude of sins, and Christine's love covered my faults, my shortcomings, and my sins. And now, even in her passing and transitioning to the next dimension of glory, she has overwhelmed me with her love. Christine Lowe was and forever will be the love of my life.

Josh:

As I reflect back on my mother, I see her smile. I hear her laugh...she always carried with her a vibrant and attractive spirit of joy. And she seemed to have this undeniable gratifying charisma about her unlike any other. In many ways, my mother was already an angel. She was an earthly angel placed here by God to minister to the hearts of those she met. And to minister she did so effortlessly with God's love...

To me my mother in many ways was a superhero. She was my superhero, and I believe that if she had a superhero name it would be The Connector. Mom, she always loved to connect with people. But I realize now the true connection was never really with the people that she encountered but with their hearts that she touched.

Serenity:

To many she was Christine, Mama Lowe, Ms. Lowe to some, Chris to others. But to me she was *Mom*. A woman of divine grace that came into my life at a very difficult time and changed my life in so many wonderful ways. She taught me the power of the Word, what it means to be a God-fearing woman. I was always fascinated with her. Her style, her unique personality. How she touched everyone she came in contact with and how she entered into a room and lit it with joy. She just had that aura about herself that attracted people. She was bold. I mean BOLD...

My beloved powerhouse. Thank you for touching my heart and my life.

Me:

Christine Lowe. She truly liberated others by being herself unapologetically. Just like she encouraged me to reach for my dreams and be my best self, she encouraged others to do the same. She used to tell us, "Use all the gifts God gave you."

I realized at a really young age how special she was, and a love like hers shouldn't be kept to just myself. That's why I didn't mind when it came to my friends or just other people that she would tell me about meeting that she would consider a daughter or son. I didn't mind that she called them a daughter or son because that's just who she was. And who am I to stop her from sharing or using all of her gifts?

My mother was my best friend, confidante, and my rider. She used to say, "We gonna ride this to the wheels fall off, girl!"

She called me her sunshine, but she brought so much warmth and light to so many others. It's said that we are called to be the hands and feet of Jesus, and that's what she was.

The thing that I admired most about her is her relationship with God. Her relationship with God was like no other. I just always used to look up to her.

Don't pity us because we've had such a wonderful life with her. I am proud and honored to say that she was mine, that she was ours...

Well done, Mom. Well done.

As we each gave our eulogy, there were tears, smiles, and laughter. After experiencing what I know is the hardest loss for all of us, we showed that by coming together we could push through the grief and survive.

FINDING STRENGTH IN SORROW

That week of planning my mother's funeral was like one

surreal moment after another. Each day consisted of making calls, running errands, and trying my best to keep it together. I didn't give myself a lot of time to grieve. I finished a task and moved on to the next. That was my coping mechanism.

Amidst the planning and gut-wrenching grief that I tried my best to ignore, I found strength, joy, and peace. I was experiencing the worst that I could imagine and yet I wasn't broken. I found strength in my faith and absolute certainty that Mom was in a better place with no more pain and sorrow. And I found joy in sharing stories with my family about the life she led and the undeniable mark she left on our lives. But the most profound thing I discovered during that week was a peace beyond understanding.

Philippians 4:7 is a Scripture that I'd always been quite familiar with: "And the peace of God, which transcends all understanding, will guard your hearts and your minds in Christ Jesus" (NIV). I'd heard it so many times over the years, and I'd experienced peace in different ways throughout my life, but never in such a profound way like I did during that week. God's peace cushioned my grief and allowed me to find the strength I needed. As Paul so adequately put it in 2 Corinthians 4:8, I was "afflicted in every way, but not crushed; perplexed, but not driven to despair" (ESV).

QUESTIONS TO CONSIDER

I draw my strength from God. If not for my faith and family,
I don't know how I would have survived.

Where do you draw your strength from?

How do you cope when life gets rough?

CHAPTER 9
THE AFTERMATH

"What is grief, if not love persevering?"[1]
— WandaVision

Grief is tricky. It's subtle and overpowering all at once. It gives no warnings and has a way of knocking you over when you least expect it.

Daniel was leaving to go back to Maryland. He'd extended his emergency leave to be with me for the funeral, but now the military was calling him back. Although I was riding on the high of experiencing God's peace, my haphazardly built armor was starting to crack, and wisps of grief began to sneak in.

I've always considered myself to be a strong woman, but my husband's quiet strength greatly contributed to holding me together. I was staying behind for another week to help Dad, and I wasn't sure how I was going to do it without Daniel. As I hugged him goodbye, I couldn't help but to cry as I already started to feel a little lost.

---

1   *WandaVision. 2021. Season 1, episode 8, "Previously On." Directed by Matt Shakman. Aired February 26, 2021.*

That first week after the funeral was a test of strength. No one tells you how businesslike death becomes after the funeral. There were calls to be made and papers to file, and somehow, you're supposed to find the strength to hold it all together to get it done.

Dad was by no means helpless, but he was accustomed to Mom handling the details of things. What do you do when it all falls on you? I took it upon myself to fill in the holes.

"Dad, do you know when you're going to get the death certificate?"

"Have you called about Mom's life insurance?"

"Have we decided on a gravestone?"

It was a never-ending list of questions and tasks, but Momma didn't raise no quitter, so I put on my proverbial big girl panties and got to work.

Amid the business, we continued to find moments to reminisce. Every night we stayed up going through pictures laughing about the good times and tearing up over our loss. Mom's absence was sorely felt. There were times when I retreated to my room just to have a moment alone when I felt my armor cracking. I was doing my best to manage a balancing act of grief and strength. Like an iceberg, the tears I did cry during that first week were just the tip of what lay beneath.

THE MELTDOWN

Soon after Daniel left, Serenity also had to return to her military duty. I was the next to leave Dad. I felt like I was abandoning him when he needed us most. I knew that I needed to return to my life, but nothing felt right anymore, and after losing one parent, I didn't want to let Dad out of my sight. It didn't matter that Josh was staying behind to be with him another week. Life had dealt a huge blow, and I couldn't help but to feel anxious over my dad.

As Josh drove me to the airport, my precarious balancing act began to slowly tip further into grief. My strength was leaving me. I began to cry quietly as we drove out of our neighborhood, realizing that the next time I came home, Mom wouldn't be there waiting. It was a subtle yet staggering realization.

Only a month into the COVID-19 pandemic, and the airport was a ghost town. I couldn't help but to think that the emptiness matched some of what I was feeling inside. Nothing was the same. I couldn't even rely on everyday life to give me some normalcy. The plane was so empty and quiet that I could practically hear my thoughts shouting at me. My only escape was sleep, but despite my exhaustion it evaded me. I was just ready to be at home with my husband in my bed.

When Daniel picked me up, I was relieved to be back in his arms, but I could feel the impending takeover of my emotions. It's as if the reserve of my strength was coming to a swift end, and grief was preparing itself to fully envelop me.

"Do you want something to eat?" Daniel asked.

"No, I just want to go home. I'm so tired," I replied. Now that my strength was leaving me, my body felt like it was shutting down.

When we arrived home, I immediately got into bed. Daniel made sure I was okay and left me to get some sleep…

but sleep did not come. Instead, a tidal wave of grief swept me under the surface. The full reality of the loss of my mother slammed into me, and I could no longer hold back the gut wrenching sobs I'd been holding in for over a week.

"Daniel…" I weakly called out. I needed him to take this pain away. My heart felt as if it was being crushed.

"Daniel!" I shouted as the waves of grief got higher and higher.

I got out of bed to find him, and when I did, I was a sobbing mess. He jumped up immediately and guided me back to the bedroom. As we lay in bed together, I desperately clung to him.

"She's gone!" I wailed into his chest.

"Breathe, honey," Daniel said soothingly as I gasped for air.

The balancing act was over. Strength was nowhere to be found, and the tip of the iceberg had completely melted to reveal the boulder of pain I was hiding underneath the surface.

TAKE CARE OF YOU

There is nothing wrong with showing strength in times of weakness. If not for my faith, I would not have been able to show the strength that I did in the immediate aftermath of my mother's death. But taking on the role of being strong for everyone else is not wise. I wanted to be what my family needed after Mom's passing, but in a way, I was neglecting myself. Everyone must deal with their own pain, no matter how badly we may want to help others. If you find yourself being strong for others, make sure there is someone in your corner being strong for you too.

LONG TERM EFFECTS

April 2020

How do you deal with grief during a pandemic? There was nowhere for me to run and hide from the pain. All I had was time to sit and think. If you're not careful, it can drive you insane. I was no longer working, so I spent a lot of time eating and watching Netflix (as I'm sure many of you did). When I was bored of that and my grief was overwhelming, I cried and poured my heart out to Daniel as I dealt with what felt like debilitating grief at times and tried my best not to regret some of my last moments with Mom.

To be honest, I was completely lost. Before Mom's passing, I had a pretty clear idea of what I wanted to do with my life. I was getting my MBA, working in marketing, and figuring out what kind of business I wanted to start on my own. We knew that we were moving to Hawaii for Daniel's new duty station, but with the pandemic we had no idea when it would happen. Now with Mom gone, I no longer wanted any of those things. Nothing made sense anymore.

But it was also in this first month that I had the idea to write this book.

Writing has always been my saving grace. When the thoughts in my head get too loud, there's nothing like feverishly writing in a journal to get it all out. The white pages don't judge you. They just allow you to expunge yourself of all the hurt and pain, but they also allow you to dream. So as I embarked on my grief journey, I took up my pen and began to write.

April 20, 2020 – Journal Entry

It's been 4 weeks since Mom passed. Last week it hit me that it's been the longest I've ever gone without communicating with her...and that is my new reality. Last night that reality made me feel like I couldn't breathe. Thank God for Daniel always being there to hold me. For the last couple of nights, I haven't been able to sleep. I think it's a combination of my sleeping patterns being thrown off and thoughts of Mom and ideas floating in my mind. I have so many wishes...I wish I could see her again. I wish I could hug her and tell her how much I love her. I wish I gave her the grandkids she wanted. I wish I visited her more. I wish I wasn't so angry with her on my second to last visit and I hope she didn't feel that anger. The list goes on and on. But I'm still just so grateful that I got to call her Mom, that she was mine and I was hers. No one knows what heaven is like, but I truly hope that we will be reunited, and my spirit will recognize hers. How do you move on when such a big part of your life is gone? These are the things I think about while lying in bed.

My life was made better because of her. And I hope to one day be as loving and gracious as she was. I miss my best friend, my confidant, my rider. I hate to cry, but crying is just a part of life for me now. I try not to ask God too many questions. We're not always meant to know the answers. But I still wonder... why couldn't she stay longer? What happened to 30 more years? How come we didn't get the miracle we were looking for? I try not to dwell too long on the questions. I still believe in God. I still have faith and hope. I trust that God knows what He is doing. And I look forward to the good that will come out of this. Death is a part of life, and it makes life that much sweeter. As humans, we're scared of death. We don't like to talk or even think about it. But to be absent from the body is to be with the Lord. I want to run my race well like Mom did. I want to be a devoted disciple and I want to learn from her life and live up to my fullest potential. This isn't just for me, but this is for her and my family and the child(ren) we will have. Ultimately, all for God.

May 2020

The first Mother's Day without Mom. I avoided social media like the plague. Seeing everyone happy with their moms? No, thank you.

I sought help. I needed someone to help me navigate the choppy waters I was in, so I called a counselor. For me, it was one of the best decisions I made to help me cope with my loss. There was a freedom in talking to someone who had no personal connection with my mother. I could air out my grievances and regrets without shame. It was the start of finding lasting peace.

May 10, 2020 – Journal Entry

The first Mother's Day without mom. I wasn't sure how I would feel today. Usually I would've talked to you, told you how much I love you, asked you how you liked your card and made sure you were having a good day. But today I couldn't do any of that. I'm grateful that today isn't as hard as I thought it would be. Momma Allen called me yesterday to check on me. And Mrs. Covington and Grandma called me today. I'm grateful that I have mother figures in my life. And of course I talked to Daniel's mom today. But the person I want to talk to the most is you, Mom. Since I can't, I'll just settle for this...

Thank you for being the best mom. Thank you for always loving me despite my flaws and being patient with me. Thank you for growing with me. I know it was hard for you to let go over the years but I think you did very well. Thank you for always believing in me and encouraging me to chase after my dreams. Thank you for pushing me to be better. Thank you for being such a great influence in my life and inspiring me to do great things. Thank you for being a spiritual guide. Thank you for always praying for me. Thank you for being a listening ear and true friend. Thank you for telling me when I was wrong and never shying away from correcting me. You made me a better person. I am who I am today because you were an exceptional mother. I'm glad that you knew how much I loved you. And I will continue to love you until the very end. You were a phenomenal woman and I hope with each passing year that I become more like you because there is no greater honor for me than to know that you continue to live through me. I love you forever and always.

Your Sunshine

June-July 2020

I needed a break from the apartment. From binging Netflix and reading my Kindle. From constantly feeling grief. The good news was Daniel had finally gotten a new move date to Hawaii. I took this as an opportunity to escape. Getting out of my day-to-day routine of nothingness was the only thing to get me sane. So, I used our impending move as an excuse to visit family. I drove to Virginia to stay with my cousins and visit a Navy friend who had just given birth to my goddaughter. It was refreshing to experience new life after death.

Going back to Maryland after my visit felt like the walls were closing in, so when Dad told me he was going to Atlanta to visit my cousin, I quickly booked a ticket and met him there. Plus, my high school best friends lived just an hour from my cousin, so it was the cherry on top. Escape was my pain reliever.

It was my cousin in Atlanta who had advised me that I should visit my mother that November before her death. During this trip with my dad, as we sat and reflected with her, I realized she saw all the signs of my mother's pending end. As a practicing nurse, she had the knowledge and experience to understand what I could not grasp. She had also experienced the death of her own father, so she knew what to look for.

Her telling me to go home was her delicate way of trying to tell me that the end was near. But my faith (and maybe even refusal to see) was keeping me from seeing the truth. Although, I'm glad I didn't see it. My mother didn't need us crying and filled with despair. She needed strength and unfailing hope.

June 9, 2020 – Journal Entry

Last week Daniel got the new date for our move to Hawaii. We will be there by August. Less than two months to get things together and move across the world. Before Mom passed and the world was put on pause, I was excited for this move. Although I did have concerns about being so far from my mom. Now that excitement has dimmed. My mom is not here to share in the excitement. I can no longer look forward to her visiting us in HI. And now my concerns are shifted to being so far from my dad. I'm sad that I can't call my mom to tell her all the little details. This is the first big change in my life that she won't be here for. The person I would call to talk through this major change is not here. I'm scared now. I can admit that I now have fears that weren't there before. I feel inadequate and a part of me feels lost. I'm moving so far from everyone I know. No job, different time zone, no friends or family nearby. A part of me already feels alone and we're not even there yet. I have no clue what to do once we settle in HI, and that scares me. I don't want to make the mistake of just settling for anything, but I also don't want to be idle. Daniel tells me I'm in a great position: no one to answer to and plenty of time with no stress for the need to make money so I can figure out what and how I want to do things. When looking at it from that perspective, I can admit that he is right. But it doesn't stop me from having these feelings of uncertainty. And amidst all that is the sadness that my mom is not here to reassure me. She's not here to cheer me on, to pray with me, to lecture me or even tell me I'm being dramatic. She's just not here. And the awareness of having to experience life changes without her is a heavy weight on my heart.

End of July

We were finally leaving Maryland to start our journey to Hawaii. But first we drove to Texas so Daniel could spend a week with his family. I convinced him to make an overnight stop in Memphis so I could see my dad again. As we drove into my hometown, I began to sob at the realization that this was the first time I was returning home and Mom wouldn't be there. Grief had snuck up on me once again.

August 2020

Almost three weeks later and we were still in Texas. The pandemic had put an indefinite pause on our travel plans. I had become somewhat of a hermit, and I felt like I was losing my mind. I wasn't happy and there was nowhere for me to go to escape it. Daniel and I had been given his little sister's room to stay in, and I spent a lot of my time in that room watching K-dramas and trying my best to avoid my in-laws. Seeing his family happy and whole was like a dagger to my heart and a constant reminder that my family was no longer whole. A slight depression was starting to sink in. I was no longer being counseled and there was no one to talk to without me feeling like I was being a party pooper.

My avoidance was starting to put a strain on my marriage. Daniel couldn't understand why I wasn't willing to spend time with his family, and all I wanted to do was retreat further within myself. I was homesick and lonely even though I was constantly surrounded by people. There was nothing he could do to make me feel better, so, much to his frustration, I flew home for a week to spend time with my dad. However, before I left, my mother-in-law eased my mind in letting me know that she understood my grief and need to go home since she had lost her dad at the age of 21. Grief is the club no one wants to join, but once you're in, it binds you together.

August 13, 2020 – Journal Entry

We have been in Texas for 2 ½ weeks. A week over what was originally planned. I have slowly become miserable in that time. And it's causing a rift between me and Daniel. His family is great but constantly being around them makes the loss of my mom and the rift between my dad and Josh all the more obvious in my life. It hurts and Daniel doesn't understand that. I feel alone. His time and attention is divided among his family and it leaves me feeling lonely. It also makes me want to go home to see my family again. I've tried talking to Daniel, but we just get frustrated with one another. With things being so delayed in the Navy, we are expected to be on hold for at least another week. I'm going home to Memphis this weekend. But I don't want to leave on a bad note with Daniel. I realize that I haven't been depending on God. No devotions or praying; that inner turmoil is evidence of what I believe. So I think I need to take the time to fortify myself alone so that I can be ready for the journey ahead. I love my husband, but this isn't something he can help me with, only God can.

September 2020

We finally left for Hawaii. I was ready, if only to get back to being just me and Daniel. And we had nothing but time since we were immediately placed into two weeks of quarantine in a Navy hotel. Isolation had slowly become a comfort to me, so I didn't mind the quarantine. It was a time to regroup and figure out what I wanted my life to look like. Ultimately, I realized that I had no clue what I was doing and despite my usual need for control, I found that a part of me was okay with that.

October 2020

We lived in that hotel for a little over a month, waiting to move into a house. I was so over feeling like an orphan with no home. From losing my mother to living out of suitcases for three months, my patience had run out. My soul was tired, and I just wanted a place to settle in and call home.

> October 23, 2020 – Journal Entry
>
> *Earlier this week we finally moved into our new home. At first, I was skeptical about this house, but now that we're here and I've started decorating I feel some sense of settled-ness that I haven't felt in a while. We ask God for things and He delivers, but because it's not exactly what we had in mind we tend to complain and lose sight of our blessing. And God has definitely blessed us.*
>
> *Of course, I can't help but to think of Mom. I miss her during this whole process. I wish I could pick up the phone to call her and tell her about every little thing. Plan for her and Dad to visit. It would*

be so nice to hear her voice and listen to her scold me about not trying to do everything at once. I just miss her presence in my life. But I was reminded in my reading this morning that she is in a way better place. Her suffering has come to an end, and she is experiencing unspeakable joy. And while I am so hurt that she is no longer here, it brings me joy to know she is with our Heavenly Father. Thank you, God, for her life and this journey I'm on.

November 2020

My 30th birthday was quickly approaching in December, and I found myself questioning life a lot. I had been looking forward to what I thought would be a milestone year, yet at the same time I feared walking into a new decade without the guidance of my mother.

On the other hand, we'd only been in Hawaii for almost two months, and I'd already found a church for us to attend. Inspire Church and the people I met there were like a balm to my soul. I had found my people, and my grief journey became a little more bearable.

November 30, 2020 – Journal Entry
Dear Mom,
My 30th birthday is in 6 days and I can't help but to think of you. What a milestone, and the fact that you're not here to see it and help me celebrate makes me sad. We were going to travel together. Now I'm making the best of the cards I've been dealt. I hope you're proud of me, and of the woman I'm continuing to become. I'm going to miss getting a birth-

day card from you and simply talking with you. I miss your godly counsel and I wonder what you would have shared with me for this next chapter in my life. To hear your voice and hug you again would be the greatest present. I will carry you everywhere with me. In every high and low. In every adventure and new endeavor. In every joy and sadness. You are an integral part of me. I don't know if you realized how much. Despite the sadness that lingers, I couldn't walk into this milestone without acknowledging you. Rest well, Mom, and I'll celebrate for the both of us.

Love, Your Sunshine

One Year Down

They say time flies when you're having fun. It also flies when you're in pain. Although, that first year wasn't all grief, it was a cocktail of mixed emotions and experiences. I discovered an awe for the great outdoors. I made new friends and gained a mentor. I turned 30. I got the dream dog I always wanted, a goldendoodle named Sunny. My relationship with Serenity was restored. Dad and I were closer than ever. Daniel went on deployment, leaving me alone for three months. I sought counseling again when Dad told me and Josh that he was seeing someone. I got a new job. Life just kept right on rolling and, somehow, we had survived the first year without Mom.

March 24, 2021 – Journal Entry
Dear Mom,
One year without you. It's still surreal some-times that you're not here with us. I think of you every

single day. Thank you for leaving the very best parts of yourself in me and the family. I wouldn't change anything about the time we had together. All of our ups and downs made me the person I am today, and I am overwhelmingly grateful for the integral part you played in shaping me. I still miss your presence and that won't go away, but as the kingdom warrior you always proclaimed me to be, I must soldier on. My love for you burns just as fiercely as if you were still here and it always will. Your grandchildren will know how wonderful, kind and amazing their "Bella" was and that she loved them greatly even though you aren't able to be in their lives. One year. It's crazy! So much has happened and many times I've wished that I could talk to you, but you've been with me every step of the way. You may not be physically here but your love and guidance is present in my life every day. Thank you for being selfless and for being love personified. You were the best mom I could've ever hoped or prayed for. I love you forever and always.

Love, Your Sunshine

Year Two

Things were going well. I was another year older, successfully made it through Daniel's second deployment, and passed my real estate license exam. Before I knew it, two years had gone by since the passing of my mom.

March 24, 2022 – Journal Entry

Today marks two years without Mom. She's always on my mind in some way. Maybe not as much as when she first passed, but she's there. Last year I had a sense of overwhelming gratefulness for the life she lived. Today I feel a calmness. I thought about crying, but I don't feel the need for that. There is just a reassurance that she is more than okay and that makes me so happy. I listened to her recording "trust issues" this morning, and it never fails to amaze me how strong she was. She said it was an honor and a privilege to be chosen by God. She never cursed Him or blamed God. She leaned into Him even more. That gives me the strength to push forward and it's a great reminder that in my weakness, God is strong. I am encouraged to obey God, use my gifts and trust that He will guide me through every circumstance. Mom, what an inspiration you are. I think she would be proud of me. Thank you, God, for blessing me with Christine Lowe.

It would also be in this second year that one of my worst fears reared its ugly head. No one warned me about the fear of losing my father. As an adult you know your parents won't always be around. But when a parent dies earlier than you expect them to, there is an almost irrational fear of losing the other parent. In my first year of grief, that fear was ever-present, but as life steadily moved along into the second year, that fear decreased...until the car accident.

Losing one parent is agonizing, but the potential to lose both in a short amount of time is unfathomable. On a Sunday afternoon, my world was flipped on its axis once again when I received a call from my father.

"Jalesa, I need you to pray," Dad gasped. "I've just

been in an accident!"

I was floored. My heart beat erratically as I tried my best to stay calm.

"Daniel!" I shouted. I felt as if I was having an out of body experience. I could barely catch my breath as I tried to form words to pray, but the only thing I could say was "Jesus!" over and over again. My only thought was that I couldn't lose Dad too, but I fought through my panic, found my strength, and rallied the troops together once again. I called family and friends asking them to pray.

Miraculously, despite the physical pain he inevitably felt from the air bags, my father walked away with no injuries, and I have no one to thank for that but God.

Oh, and the someone that my dad told me he was seeing a year prior? She played a major role in easing my mind when it came to his recovery from the pain.

April 11, 2022 – Journal Entry

Yesterday, one of my biggest fears almost came to light. Dad called me saying he was in a car accident. Ever since Mom passed, I've had this fear of losing Dad. Every day we wake up is a miracle. Every time we leave home and return safely, it's a blessing. Mom passing made life seem all the more fragile and precious, and it made me want to hold on to Dad all the more. Mom went way too soon and I'm afraid of the possibility of that happening to Dad. I know the "when" is completely out of my control. It's all up to God, but it doesn't stop me from feeling the way I do. Dad was completely shaken when he called me, which shook me up too. He asked me to pray, but how do you pray when your worst fear is being realized??? As I tried to pray the only words I could really think or say are "God, please, Jesus, be with him." In that moment Daniel came through for me in saying a full prayer. Also, for the first time I was truly grateful for Veronica's presence in my dad's life. Ultimately, Dad is fine, and I thank God for shielding and protecting him. He walked away without a scratch. Once again, it is proven to me that life is fragile, but God is still good.

A lot has changed in the time since Mom's been gone. I visited home after almost three years of being gone. Everything has changed, yet nothing is different. My childhood home still holds the warmth of memories, but it looks different now that Dad has begun to renovate. The familiar faces of family and friends still welcome me, yet there is an unfamiliar face in the crowd in the form of my dad's girlfriend.

Time waits for no one, and I've learned to keep pressing forward and enjoy what this life has to offer.

GRIEF IS A JOURNEY

Much like life, grief is not linear. It is like a roller coaster with many dips and spins—except nothing about it is thrilling. I was on a new path with no directions, trying to make sense of my mother's death.

I've heard the aftermath of grief described as stages. As if you could safely make your way through a quick and tidy process and arrive at healing. From my experience, this is not the case. I've found that grief is more of a journey. There is nothing straightforward about it. At times it is a snarling beast that attacks you at random. Other times, it is a quiet pain that hides in the subconscious.

Of course, in the beginning my grief was ever present, but as I have learned to cope, I have grown to appreciate the life my mother lived instead of mourning the time I lost with her. However, there are times when my grief overwhelms me. It sneaks into my dreams, invades my happy moments, and makes my sad moments seem even more dire at times.

For those of you who wonder if grief ever ends, I regret to inform you that I don't think it will. You learn to live with it instead. That doesn't mean that life will be depressing (unless you allow it). Instead, I think of it as a reluctant companion in life, but one that has made me stronger. So as I continue in this life, I welcome the grief that reminds me of the bright light that was my mother and her lasting influence on my journey.

QUESTIONS TO CONSIDER

How have you handled your grief and pain?

Are you allowing yourself to feel or are you in denial?

In what ways are you expressing your grief? There are healthy and unhealthy ways to express ourselves. Make sure you're not causing more damage to yourself or others around you while processing your grief.

CHAPTER 10
SURVIVING

*And we know that God causes everything to work
together for the good of those who love God and
are called according to His purpose for them.*
— Romans 8:28 (NLT)

So how do you survive when the miracle you prayed for,
hoped for, *believed for* doesn't happen? To be honest, I'm
still figuring it out. But one thing I know is that God never
promised us this life would be easy. Instead, after we have
suffered, He "will himself restore, confirm, strengthen, and
establish" us (1 Peter 5:10).

Rather than being angry at God for what others may
deem an unfair tragedy in life, I look for the lessons and
blessings. Because if there's nothing else I've learned in this
life, it's that there is always a lesson to be learned and a
blessing to receive in every situation, whether it's apparent
now or later.

1. **Life Is Short**

This is such a cliché, but it has never been truer and something that I became painfully aware of when my mom passed. She died at 58! I remember when I was a child, I thought 30 was old! Now in my early 30s, it is clear to me that we could leave this earth at any moment. We have all experienced it in some degree as COVID-19 has completely shaken the whole world with its death toll.

My mother had plans to travel the world. She'd lived her whole life in Tennessee, but she'd always had a desire to move somewhere else. She believed that it was time for her to make a change in her life, not only in where she lived but also in her daily habits. She'd struggled with some health issues, but nothing that ever made us think that she would die so soon in life.

My mother and I had plans together. We would see Greece together. When she retired, she and Dad would move to the same city as me and Daniel. We talked about what kind of mother I would be to my future children and how she would spoil them. We had plans, but none of those things will happen.

The Bible says in Proverbs 19:21 that "you can make many plans, but the Lord's purpose will prevail" (NLT). Now some may read that and think, *Well, what's the point of planning anything if God's just going to do what He wants in the end?!* But I read this Scripture and understand that because life is short it is paramount that we know our purpose in life and follow the plans God has for us. It doesn't mean that we don't plan and just leave things up to chance. That's the last thing we should do! However, we must plan and allow God to guide us in those plans. Everything may not happen the way we expect it to, and that's okay! We must readjust and don't let fear or sorrow keep us from living this short yet beautiful life.

2. **Get Help**

As I mentioned before, my mom was always an advocate for counseling. She understood that seeking counseling looked like a sign of weakness, but it actually showed strength. In the African American community, we are often taught to keep our problems to ourselves. "If it ain't broke, don't fix it!" But what if we hide from our problems so much that we begin to believe that we don't have any problems at all? That can become a dangerous thing. We harm ourselves without even realizing it.

Within a month of my mom passing, I sought help. It was the beginning of COVID, I was stuck in the house, and I had nothing but time to think about my loss. I had never experienced grief before, and I was lost as to how to process it. Daniel tried his best to be there for me, but I felt a disconnect at times when trying to explain to him how I felt. So, I asked myself what would my mother do? She would get help! I've sought counseling twice since her passing, and I know I'll need it in the future.

Isolation and not asking for help are the quickest ways to drown in your pain. Don't let loss keep you from seeking the help you need. Let people be there for you. Surround yourself with people who love you unconditionally. Whether they understand what you're going through or not, it's those who love you most who will pull you out of the darkness. And the professionals are there to help you process in a way that is healthy. People say that it takes a village to raise a child, but it also takes a village to sustain life. We weren't meant to walk this earth alone, so go and get the help you need.

3. **Find Your Purpose**

Why am I here? What is my purpose? What do I want people to say about me when I'm no longer here? I've asked myself these questions and similar ones many times over the years. I've started and stopped many paths in my short life. Some paths I saw to the end and others I realized were not for me. Before my mom's passing, I was on a path that included an MBA, working in marketing and eventually starting my own business. After her passing, everything came to a standstill. I no longer knew what I wanted or what I should be doing.

My mind was chaos, and I soon realized that a lot of my identity was wrapped up in my mom. But with her no longer here, I had to figure out who I was without her. Mom had fulfilled her purpose in life. I truly believe that for those of us who are still here, it is because we have things we need to accomplish.

Mom's life may have ended sooner than I wanted or than she expected, but I have no doubt in my mind that she did what she was meant to do.

Your loved one may have passed, but you still have work to do! As much as it hurts, life continues long after our loved ones have passed on. It is a waste to live life in despair mourning for someone who is no longer. Make their lives count! What did his/her life teach you? What message did their lives leave behind? Learn what you can from it and find your message. God says in Jeremiah 29:11, "For I know the plans I have for you...they are plans for good and not for disaster, to give you a future and a hope" (NLT). Lean into your purpose and live the life that God is calling you to.

4. **Regret Is a Silent Killer**

Should've, could've, would've. We have all said them, right? They are the regrets that we torture ourselves with. When my mom passed there were so many things that I wish I'd done differently. Sometimes my dad and I would talk and go over those last few months with her. Was there anything we could have done differently? Did we show her enough love? Did we ask the doctors enough questions? Were there other options we didn't consider? Should we have just let her come home?

It was a daily battle for me in the beginning not to torture myself with constant questions. I felt that maybe I hadn't done enough and that thought alone filled me with regret. As I was trying to heal, regret found ways to kill the peace I had in knowing Mom was in a better place. Eventually, with the help of counseling, I had to learn that no matter how much I may wish for things to be different, there is no going back. We cannot change the past so we must make peace with it. And I know that there was no doubt in my mother's mind of how much we loved her because, in the end, love was all we had to assure her.

At some point in life, everyone has regrets, but I urge you not to wallow in them. It's a dangerous game to play. We can't live in the past, moaning and groaning about missed chances. Because while you're doing that, you're missing out on the present and possibly creating more regrets. Instead, live in the now, learn for tomorrow and get better.

5. **Continue the Legacy**

Christine Clark Lowe was a giver, a peacemaker, and a phenomenal mother. She never met a stranger and she made anyone who came within her sphere feel seen and heard. She was gracious and kind and a complete joy to be around. I also liked to call her the silent storm, but when you angered her, she never yelled. Instead, she just had this way of looking at you and you knew that there'd be consequences. I'm trying my best to replicate that look by the time I have kids!

Ultimately, my mother was a woman after God's heart. I aspire to be like her.

Years from now, I will continue to tell her

story. I will tell of the woman who may not have been well-known to the world but was known and loved in her world. She made an impact on hundreds of people from young to old. She may not have been able to make all her plans and dreams come true, but I will carry the baton forward. I will show that same love for people that she had. I will continue to nurture our family as she would have. I will thank God for every blessing and tribulation as she would have. And I will not only survive but thrive, as she taught me to do.

When our loved ones move on from this earth, we cannot lay down and die with them. We are meant to carry on, fulfill our purpose and leave behind a legacy just as our loved ones did for us. What do you want people to say about you when you're gone? Now is the time to start building that legacy.

A FINAL WORD

I learned and am still learning to relinquish *all* my control and put my full trust in God, especially when things aren't looking good. Because despite my loss, I am immensely grateful that God blessed me. You may be thinking to yourself, *What kind of blessing could she have possibly gotten from losing her mother?!* Well, I'll tell you. In her last year of her life, my mom and I formed an even tighter bond and shared so many precious moments. I wouldn't trade the time I spent with her and the conversations we had for anything. She taught me so much about life and how to live it in that one year, and she blessed me with a mother's love that will last a lifetime.

No one knows when his/her time is done on this earth. The beauty and pain of life and death is that life goes on after death. Sometimes, you may wish you could go back after experiencing such a deep loss, but that's impossible. I fully believe that my mother is in heaven pain-free and joyful. As much as I would love to have one more day or even just a moment with her, I know she's where she needs to be. So instead, I hold on tight to the years of memories I have with her. That is why I believe that time is the most precious commodity. It's the memories of time spent with our loved ones that we hold dear, and one thing I can say without a doubt is that my family has many memories with Mom that we will forever cherish.

So be encouraged, my friend! Go out and live life! Make memories with the ones you love, fulfill your purpose, and remember that even if the miracle doesn't happen, you're a survivor and life is still worth living.

And now, I'll leave you with words from my mother:

Recording from December 13, 2019 — The day I flew home and surprised her.

"It's an honor. Oh, my gracious. *It's an honor.* It's a real honor to be chosen. To be used by You. Thank you, Heavenly Father, for trusting me with this trial. Thank you, Jesus Christ, for loving me so much that you died on that cross for me. And then you didn't stay there. I thank you that you are seated at the right hand of the Father. Father, Son, and the Holy Spirit comes into agreement, has mapped out a plan for my life…and everything that will come after me. Father, I thank you. What an honor and a privilege."

What an honor and privilege to have had Christine

Clark Lowe as my mother, and to know that I will continue her legacy and bring glory to God in the process.

"I press on toward the goal to win the prize for which God has called me heavenward in Christ Jesus."

— Philippians 3:14 (NIV)

ACKNOWLEDGEMENTS

First, giving thanks to God. This book truly was not my idea! I was fresh in my grief when I heard God whisper the title of this book to me. If it weren't for God, you would not be holding this book in your hands. And I'm so grateful to Him for using me to get this story out.

To my husband: Thank you for seeing me through the hardest time in my life. Your love and unfailing support have been the constant I needed to make it through. You listened to me as I ranted and rebelled against God when I didn't want to write, and you never judged me. I love you.

To my dad: Thank you for being you Papa Bear. In the aftermath of losing mom, our relationship has been one of the things I cherish most in this life.

To my brother and sister: You two are the best siblings I could ask for. I'm grateful we've been able to establish a tighter bond.

To my church family: The people I met at Inspire Church in Hawaii were my saving grace as I struggled to write this book. There are so many who encouraged me, and I wish I could thank you all personally, but here are a few who made a great impact.

-Pastor Ju you were an answered prayer when I felt lost after my mother's death. I can always count on your spiritual guidance to push me out of my comfort zones. I can say without a doubt that if it hadn't been for your mentorship, this book wouldn't be a reality.

- To the ladies of my mentorship group, our year of weekly fellowship has grown me in a way that I never expected. I'm grateful to each of you for the constant encouragement and believing in me to make this happen.

- Deja and Chelsea, you ladies were the first who I let read my rough drafts. Your constructive criticism was so needed! I really appreciate you.

- Finally, Janine. We connected because we both experienced loss due to cancer. And we connected on our passion projects. Every time I saw you, you asked me if my book was done. Thank you for that! That accountability was crucial to me following through on this book. So, I can finally say: "Here's the book!"

Thank you all!